Anonymus

Catalogue of the valuable Collection of Coins of the late Joseph J. Mickley

Anonymus

Catalogue of the valuable Collection of Coins of the late Joseph J. Mickley

ISBN/EAN: 9783742802279

Manufactured in Europe, USA, Canada, Australia, Japa

Cover: Foto ©Thomas Meinert / pixelio.de

Manufactured and distributed by brebook publishing software (www.brebook.com)

Anonymus

Catalogue of the valuable Collection of Coins of the late Joseph J. Mickley

CATALOGUE

OF THE VALUABLE

COLLECTION OF COINS

OF THE LATE

JOSEPH J. MICKLEY,

COMPRISING

Early British, English, German, Spanish, French, Italian, Swedish, Danish, Chinese and American Coins and Medals, in Gold, Silver and Copper. In each Series will be found many Fine and Rare Specimens.

Also, Valuable Numismatic Works, Continental Currency, Dies; a Collection of Curiosities, consisting of Mummies Heads, Indian War Implements, Fossils, Shakspeare's Lantern, &c., &c.

TO BE SOLD

Tuesday and Wednesday Afternoons and Evenings,

November 5th and 6th, 1878,

Commencing at 3 o'clock,

At the Auction Rooms, 139 and 141 South Fourth St.

M. THOMAS & SONS, Auctioneers.

☞ Can be examined on Monday, November 4th.
☞ Sale of Books to take place October 29th, 30th and 31st.
☞ Sale of Autographs to take place November 1st.

Sherman & Moore, Printers, 501 Chestnut Street, Phila.

NOTE.

The attention of numismatists is called to the fine condition and great variety of modern silver and copper foreign coins in the within catalogue. The late J. J. Mickley enjoyed rare opportunities (during a recent three years' tour of Europe) of collecting complete sets of this class of coins; some of which he collected by authority of the United States government, visiting for the purpose some thirty-five mints of different nations. In this way, and by purchase, a number of duplicate sets and single pieces were obtained, which form a part of this cabinet. The American series, though far from being complete, contains many rare specimens, a portion of which are in PROOF *or* UNCIRCULATED *condition. Great care has been taken to give the exact condition and rarity of the important examples in this really interesting collection. Mr. Mickley's well-known aversion to counterfeit coins, &c., is a guarantee that copies (unless of historical interest) are few and far between, and when met with, are properly described.* OVER DESCRIPTION *has been carefully avoided. Having had a rather large experience in arranging cabinets for public sale, the subscriber feels confident the present effort will prove satisfactory to all concerned.*

E. MASON, Jr.,
Numismatist.

First Day's Sale, Nos. 1 to 675.

Second Day's Sale, Nos. 676 to 1093.

The Curiosities will be sold at the conclusion of Catalogue.

SCALE OF THE NUMISMATIC SOCIETY OF PHILADELPHIA.

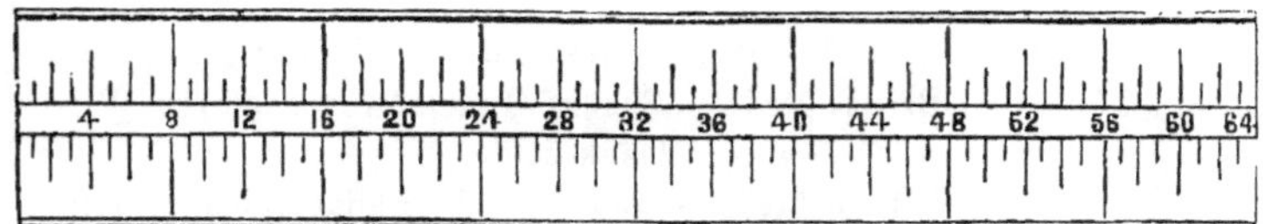

CATALOGUE.

Miscellaneous, Foreign and American Medals, Coins, &c.

COPPER.

1 Franklin Institute Scott Premium Medal, bronze proof. *Size* 35

2 Franklin Medal, (Natus, Boston;) *rev.*, Figure of Mars, bronze proof, *scarce.* *Size* 30

3 Ditto, (Natus, Boston;) *rev.* in 4 lines: "Eripuit Coelo Fulmen Sceptrum Que Tyrannis," surrounded by a Wreath, bronze, *fine, rare.* *Size* 29

4 Bronze Medal—WM. WASHINGTON for Cowpens. *Size* 29

5 Somers' American Naval Medal; *obv.*, Ship; *rev.*, Wreck, Boats, &c., bronze proof, *scarce.* *Size* 36

6 Bronze Medal—JOHN EGAR HOWARD for Cowpen's, *fine.* *Size* 29

7 Ditto, proof.

8 Bronze Medal, containing on *obv.* and *rev.*, "Chronology of the Reigns of England," proof. *Size* 32

9 Bronze United States Mint Medal—JAMES MADISON, proof. *Size* 48

10 French Bronze Medal—"Libertas Americana, Fourth of July, 1776," tarnished proof, *rare.* *Size* 30

11 Ditto.

12 Bronze Medal—GEN. LAFAYETTE; *rev.*, "the Defender of American and French Liberty, &c.;" beautiful olive proof, *rare.* *Size* 30

13 Ditto.

14 Bronze Medal—FRANKLIN and MONTYON, *fine.* *Size* 27

15 Bronze Medal; *obv.*, Bust of NAPOLEON III; *rev.*, Bust of EUGENIE, *fine, scarce.* *Size* 32

16 1868 Spanish Dollar, struck in copper, bronze proof, *rare.*

17 Bronze Medal—Bust of QUEEN VICTORIA; *rev.*, Wreath, Crown, &c., blank field. *Size* 27

18 Bronze Medal—Sanitary Fair, Philadelphia, *very fine.* *Size* 36

19 Bronze Medal—Bust of ADAM ECKFELDT, Chief Coiner United States Mint, 1814 to 1839, from Officers of the Mint, 1859, *very fine, scarce.* *Size* 32

20 Bronze Medal—Coronation of WILLIAM IV, *fine.* *Size* 29

21 Bronze Medal—GEORGE III MEMORIAL, *fine.* *Size* 26

22 Bronze Medal—GEORGE IV, Born, Died, &c., *very fine.* *Size* 27

23 Bronze Medal—GEORGE IV; *rev.*, Britannia and Hibernia Clasping Hands, *pierced.* *Size* 30

24 Bronze Medal—Coronation of GEORGE IV, *very fine.* *Size* 22

25 1870 White Metal Medal—WILHELM DER SIEGREICHE for Metz, proof. *Size* 25

26 1871 German White Metal Peace Medal, proof. *Size* 24

27 Bronze Franklin Medal—Mechanics' Literary Association, Rochester; *rev.*, Awarded to ———, *fine.* *Size* 26

28 1793 Bermuda Half Penny: *obv.*, GEORGE III; *rev.*, Ship, proof, *scarce.*

29 Token—Sheffield Constitutional Society, copper, *very fine.*

30 6 Copper Coins—Sarawak: One Cent, Half Cent and Quarter Cent, two sets, *fine, scarce.*

31 25 Copper Coins—Russian, Turkish, Greek, Italian, &c., *good condition.*

32 1797 English Two-pence, Copper, *good.*

33 Lot (12) Coins, various Nations, *good, uncirculated.*

34 White Metal Silver-plated Medal—Cathedral, Philadelphia, in papier mache box. *Size* 51

35 French Bronze Medal—FRANKLIN and MONTYON, *fine.* *Size* 25

36 White Metal Medal—QUEEN OF SWEDEN; *rev.*, Angel of Peace, proof. *Size* 28

37 1808 East India Co. Coin, copper—"XX Cash," brilliant proof in metallic case, *scarce.*

38 1797 George III Penny; *rev.*, Britannia, countersunk field, proof, in metallic box, *scarce.*

39 Foreign Copper Coins: French, Turkish, English, &c. All bright and uncirculated, 38 pieces. A beautiful lot.

40 Bronze Mint Medal—JOSEPH MADISON, proof. *Size* 32

41 Bronze Mint Medal—GENERAL HARRISON, for Battle of the Thames. *Size* 40

42 Bronze French Medal, by Dupré—PAUL JONES, *fine, scarce.* *Size* 36

43 Bronze Medal—Franklin Natus Boston. proof. *Size* 29

44 Iron Plate Medal—Bust of FRANKLIN; countersunk field, history unknown, perhaps unique, *very fine.* *Size* 52

45 Bronze Mint Medal—JOHN ADAMS, proof. *Size* 32

46 1797 White Metal Washington Medal—Presidency Relinquished, proof. *Size* 29

47 1783 White Metal Medal—Libertas Americana; *rev*, "Communi Consensu," dull proof, *fine, pierced, very rare.* *Size* 29

48 White Metal Brunel Medal; *rev.*, Thames Tunnel, proof, *scarce.* *Size* 24

49 White Metal Geary Medal, proof. *Size* 20

50 Bronze Lowell School Medal, proof. *Size* 24

51 Bronze Lafayette Medal — "Defender of American and French Liberty," &c., *very fine.* *Size* 29

52 Bronze Obituary Medal, by Pingo; *obv.*, Thos. Snelling; *rev.*, Born, Died, &c, *very fine, rare.* *Size* 25

53 Bronze Medal—WILLIAM PITT; *rev.*, "The Man who having saving the Parent, &c.," proof, *scarce.* *Size* 25

54 Bronze Medal—FRANKLIN and MONTYON, *fine.* *Size* 26

55 Bronze Medal—"Libertas Americana, Fourth of July, 1876," *very fine, rare.* *Size* 30

56 Bronze Medalette—DAVID HOSACK, M. D., *very fine.* *Size* 21

57 1797 Bronze Medal—WASHINGTON, Presidency Relinquished, proof. *Size* 29

58	1797	Bronze Medal—WASHINGTON, Presidency Relinquished, proof. *Size* 29
59	1797	Ditto.
60	1797	Ditto.
61		Bronze Medal—Bust of JESSE KETCHUM, Buffalo School, *very fine, scarce.* *Size* 30
62		Bronze Franklin Medal, by Dupré—"Natus, Boston," *fine.* *Size* 29
63		German White Metal Religious Medal, 1848, proof. *Size* 25
64		Bronze Memorial Medal—GEORGE III, *very fine.* *Size* 26
65		Bronze Humanity Medal, *size* 21; White Metal Loyalty Medal, *size* 19, proof. 2 pieces.
66		Bronze Wm. Washington Medal for Cowpens, *very fine.* *Size* 29
67	1779	Rhode Island Medal, brass, *very fine, rare.* *Size* 20
68		Carthagena Medal, brass, *fine, rare.* *Size* 24
69		Admiral Boscowen Cape Breton or Louisburg Medal, brass, *very fine, rare.* *Size* 24
70		Ditto, *fine, rare.* *Size* 15
71		18 Foreign and American Copper and Brass Coins, &c., most of them in fine condition, *some scarce.*
72	1797	Bronze Mint Medal—JOHN ADAMS, proof. *Size* 32
73	1797	Ditto.
74	1797	Ditto.
75		Bronze Medalette—West Point Military Academy, *very fine, rare.* *Size* 19
76		North Wales Piece, copper; *obv.*, GEORGIUS WASHINGTON, *good condition, scarce.*
77	1792	Coventry Half Penny; *rev.*, Nude Female Figure on Horseback, *uncirculated, bright red, scarce.*
78	1793	2 Mule Pieces; *obv*, Liberty and Commerce, 1794; *rev.*, a Stork, date beneath 1793, copper, *very fine.*
79	17—	American Colonial Copper Coin—Auctori Plebis; *rev.*, Figure of Hope, Legend Indep. et Liber., *very rare, fine.*
80	1872	2 English Silver Coins—(1 Florin,) *uncirculated.*
81		20 English and Austrian Coins, from the size of an English Shilling to an English Silver Penny, mostly Maunday Money, all uncirculated, all silver; some varieties and some duplicates.

82 Silver Medal—William Pitt; *rev.*, the Man who having saved the Parent, proof, *very rare.* *Size* 25

83 1791 Washington Cent., 1791, Large Eagle, *fine. rare.*

84 Washington Bronze Medalette—Liberty and Security, *uncirculated, thick die, rare.* *Size* 21

85 Bronze Lowell School Medal, proof, *very fine, rare.* *Size* 23

86 1793 Washington Liverpool Half Penny, *fine, scarce.*

87 1783 Washington and Independence Cent, Laureated Military Bust, copper, *scarce.*

88 1783 Washington and Independence Cent, Large Head, *scarce.*

89 Washington and Independence, English restrike, copper, proof.

90 Washington Brass Medalette—"Success to the United States," *scarce.* *Size* 18

91 Kentucky Cent, plain edge, *fine, scarce.*

92 1811 United States Copper Half Cent, restrike, *uncirculated, rare.*

93 Washington Sanitary Fair Medalette, silver proof, *very fine.* *Size* 12

94 1797 Bronze Washington Medal, Commission Resigned, proof. *Size* 29

95 1797 Ditto.

96 1797 Ditto.

97 1797 Ditto, white metal, brilliant, proof.

98 10 Small American and Foreign Silver Coins, uncirculated and proofs, *all different.*

99 3 Colonial Coins—Massachusetts, Virginia and Vermont, *all good.*

100 34 American and Foreign Copper and Brass Coins, Tokens, Store Cards, Medalettes, &c. Some in uncirculated condition, balance good; *varieties.*

101 1787 6 New York Cents—(Nova Eborac,) two very good and four very fair, *scarce.*

102 1856 United States Nickle Cent, *fine, rare.*

103 18 Nickle and Bronze United States Two and One-cent Pieces, all uncirculated, different dates.

104 1872 3 United States Nickle Cents, 15 Nickle and 20 Three-cent Pieces, *uncirculated.*

105 2 Tin Pieces—JAMES II; *obv.*, Equestrian Figure, *rare, in fair condition.*

106 Small German Copper Medalette, with Ring, for Faithful Service in two Campaigns.

107 English Token; *obv.*, Bust of Fox; *rev.*, Indian with Bow and Tomahawk; Legends, "If Rents I once consent to pay my Liberty is passed away;" proof, *scarce.*

108 1806 Bahama Half Penny; *rev.*, Ship, &c., *uncirculated, scarce.*

109 1859 Indian Head United States Cent, struck in copper, *scarce.*

110 1871 Silver Two-franc Piece, Republic; one of the first Coins of the first Payment of the French to the Germans, *rare, variety, fine.*

111 Siamese Copper Coin; *obv.*, 3 Pagodas; *rev.*, Elephant, &c., *fair, scarce.*

112 1787 Connecticut Cent, double strike, *fine.*

113 Louisbourg Silver Medal; *obv.*, Globe, surrounded by Allegorical Figures, Fame, &c.; *rev.*, Naval Battle, Legend, Louisbourg taken 1758, *very fine, very rare.* *Size* 28

114 Bronze Stony Point Medal, 15th July, 1779; *rev.*, Fort, Vessels, &c., *fine, rare.* *Size* 29

115 White Metal Medal—I. O. of O. F. Celebration, 1869, Phila., *fair.*

116 Silver Jewish Shekel, can be traced back many years, but undoubtedly a copy. *Size* 16

ANCIENT AND MODERN COPPER AND SILVER COINS, MEDALS, &c.

117 Very Curious Roman Medal, a Remarkable Specimen of the Ingenuity of the Romans, in facetiæ, brass, in fine condition, and believed to be original, *excessively rare.*

118 8 Interesting Small Silver Coins, different, some curious, *fine.*

119 Second Bronze of AUGUSTUS CÆSAR, *very good.*

120 Family Silver Coin—Pomponia; *rev.*, Wolf and Twins, *very fine, scarce.*

121 17 Coins from Pompeii, all poor, *small.*

122 Gaulish Copper Coin, *fair, rare.*

123 Gaulish Copper Coin, *rare, different variety, very good.*

124 Gaulish Copper Coin—CHIEF CRITIOUS, *fair, rare.*

125 Gaulish Copper Coin, *different variety, very fair, rare.*

126 Gaulish Silver Plated Coin, *fine, rare.*

127 Ditto, much smaller, *variety.*

☞ These small and interesting coins (122 to 127) were purchased by Mr. Mickley, from the Los Comte collection.

128 Silver Half Penny—RICHARD I, England, coined in Pictou, *fine, very rare.*

129 Copper Coin—HENRY III, England; *obv.*, King on the Throne, *fine, rare.*

130 Silver Denier—BEOMODOS; *rev.*, Antiochia, *fine, rare.*

131 Ditto—CONRAD, KING OF GENOA, *fine, rare.*

132 Silver Medalette—HERCULES, DUKE OF FAVORA, *fine, rare.* *Size* 17

133 Silver Medalette—ALFONSUS, *fine, rare, pierced.* *Size* 19

134 Huguenot Medal of GREGORY XIII, copper, *fine, rare.* *Size* 20

135 2 Swedish Medals of CHARLES XI, 1 in copper, 1 in iron, *fine, rare.* *Size* 21

136 3 Medals—WILLIAM, DUKE OF CUMBERLAND, 2 in copper, *fine rare, size* 21; 1 in bronze, *size* 27.

137 1677 1 Or, Large Copper Coin of Sweden, *good, rare.*

138 Silver Peace Medal—VERSAILLES, 1729, *very fine, rare.* *Size* 26

139 Medal Commemorating the Death of the PRINCESS CHARLOTTE, brass, gilt, *scare.* *Size* 32

140 Montreal Silver Medal—Conquest of Canada; *rev.*, "Montreal Taken, 1760," proof, *very rare.* *Size* 26

141 Silver Medal; *obv.*, "Britannia;" *rev.*, Quebec Taken, 1759, *fine, very rare.* *Size* 25

142 Silver Medal; *obv.*, Guadaloupe Surrendered, May 1st, 1759; *rev.*, Figure of Britannia, proof, *very rare.*

143 Silver Peace Medal; *obv.*, Fame Seated on Clouds, with Shield of Holland, containing 13 Stars, date 1782, fine proof, *very rare.* *Size* 29

144 Silver Peace Medal; *obv.*, 3 Figures, personifying America, Holland and Great Britain, 1782, brilliant proof. *Size* 28

145 Silver Medal struck to Commemorate the Preliminaries of Peace at Paris, and End of the Seven Years' War, 1782, proof, *very rare.* *Size* 29

146 1691–'93 German Medal, silver; *obv.*, 2 Horns of Plenty, forming a Semicircle around Views of Mining, Farming, &c., Sun at the top; Legend, "Feld, Bringt, Korn und Geldt dies Reiche;" *obv.*, inscription of 16 lines, *fine, rare.* *Size* 30

147 1871–'72 3 Two-franc and One-franc Pieces, silver—Republic of France, *uncirculated, scarce.*

148 1871–'72 Two Francs, One Franc and Half Franc—Republic of France, *uncirculated, scarce.* 3 pieces.

149 1867, '68 and '69 Five Franc, Two Franc, One Franc and Half France—NAPOLEON III, *uncirculated.* 4 pieces.

150 1866 Maximilian Dollar, *fine, scarce.*

151 1817 George III Silver Medal; *obv.*, Bust; *rev.*, 3 Figures, representing England, Ireland and Scotland, proof, *rare.* *Size* 25

152 1759 George II Quebec Medal; *obv.*, Bust; *rev.*, Crown Point, Quebec, Niagara, &c., silver, *very fine, rare.* *Size* 28

153 Curious German Copper Medal; *obv.*, Vineyard, Male Figure watering the Vine; *rev.*, Female Figures; Legend, "Die Gute Zucht, *fine:* *Size* 28

154 Silver-plated Nickel Medal, German; *obv.*, Monogram R. W., crowned; *rev.*, Wreath, Inscription "Kriegs Verdienst," proof. *Size* 24

155 1870 One Thaler—Schwarzburg, Sondershausen, silver, proof

156 California Gold Quarter and Prince Albert Medalette, Copper, *fine*, 2 pieces. *Size* 5

COINS, MEDALS, &c., OF SOUTH AMERICA.

157 1849 Set Silver Proof Coins—New Granada, 9 pieces, from Dollar to Half Dime Size, *rare.*

158 1869 Set Proof Copper Coins—Republic of Uruguay, 3 pieces, Four, Two and One Centisimo, *scarce.*

159 1869 Ditto.

160 1872 Bronze Proof Coins—Republic of Equador, Two and One Centavo, 2 pieces, *scarce.*

161 1872 Ditto.

162 1876 2 Nickle Coins, Venezuela—Two and a Half and One Centavo, *uncirculated, scarce.*

163 1860 55 Silver Brazilian Coins, 2000 Reis, 1000 Reis, 500 Reis, two 200 Reis, 5 pieces, *uncirculated.*

COINS OF MEXICO.

165 1822 Mexican Silver Iturbide Dollar; *rev.*, Eagle Resting on one Foot on Cactus, *fine, scarce.*

166 1822 Ditto, different reverse, *fine.*

167 1822 Ditto, different variety, *fine.*

168 1866 Maximilian Dollar and Half Dollar, *fine, scarce.* 2 pieces.

169 1866 Maximilian Dollar, *fine.*

170 1866 Maximilian Dollar, *very good.*

171 1870 Silver Dollar—Republic of Mexico; *rev.*, Scales, Liberty Cap, &c., *very fine, scarce.*

172 1871 Silver Dollar—Republic of Mexico, *very fine variety, scarce.*

JAPANESE AND SIAMESE COINS.

173 1875 Full Set Japanese Silver and Copper Coins, 9 silver pieces, from Dollar size to Half Dime size, 4 copper pieces; *uncirculated, scarce.* 13 pieces.

174 7 Japanese Coins—Half Cobang: 2 One-quarter Cobang, Silver Itzebue, and 2 One-quarter Itzebues; *very fine, scarce.* 4 gold and 3 silver.

175 Silver Japanese Coin—1 Itzebue, *fine.*

176 Set Old Style Japanese Silver Coins—Kodama, Gin or Bullet Money, *fine.* (50 years old.)

177 Siamese Lead or Tin Coin; *obv.*, 3 Pagodas; *rev.*, Elephant, &c., *fine, rare.* *Size* 20

178 Ditto, *very good.*

179 Ditto. 3 pieces, 2 large, 1 small, *fair.*

180 6 Ancient Spanish Silver Coins, curious and interesting, *very fair.*

181 Japanese Coin—One Cent, copper, *very fine, scarce.*

182 Ditto, Half Cent.

183 4 Siamese Coins, 1 silver and 3 copper, *very scarce, fine.*

184 2 Ancient Greek Coins—Hiero of Sicily, small, brass, *very fair, rare.*

RUSSIAN COINS.

185 1780 5 Kopec, copper, *fine.*

186 1802 5 Kopec, copper, *very good variety.*

187 1803 5 Kopec, copper, *very fine, rare variety.*

188 1803 5 Kopec, copper, *fine variety.*

189 1840 2 Kopec, copper, *fine.*

190 1867 5 Kopec, copper, proof, *scarce.*

191 1867 2 Kopec, copper, proof, *scarce.*

192 1867 2 Copper Coins, 10 Pennia, *very fine, scarce.*

193 1867 5 Copper Coins, 5 Pennia, *uncirculated.*

194 1870 Set Silver Coins, from Dollar to Half Dime in size, 7 pieces, *uncirculated.*

195 1867 Set Copper Coins, 4 pieces, proofs.

196 1860–'68 16 Silver Coins, from Half Dollar to Half Dime in size, *very fine, but few duplicates.*

197 1867 Set Copper Coins, from 5 Kopec to ¼ Kopec, 6 pieces, proof, *scarce.*

198 1870 Set Silver, Dollar to Dime in size; 4 pieces, *uncirculated, scarce.*

199 1866–'69 10 Small Copper Coins, 1 Pennia, *uncirculated.*

UNITED STATES CENTS.

200 1793 Wreath, Stars and Bars on Edge, uncirculated, beautiful olive color, sharp impression. *Very rare in this condition.*

201 1793 Chain or Link Cent, perfect die, *fine, dark color, rare.*

202 1794 Uncirculated, light olive, *small planchet.*

203 1794 Fine sharp impression, date left of Bust, *small planchet.*

204 1794 Very fine, olive color, sharp and beautiful impression, *large planchet.*

205 1794 Good condition, *small planchet.*

206 1794 Extra good variety.

207 1795 Thin Planchet, good impression, "One Cent" high in the wreath.

208 1795 Thick Planchet, lettered edge, very good, "One Cent" high in the wreath.

209 1796 Fillet Head, good, "One Cent" high in the wreath.

210 1797 Good.

211 1798 Very fine, dark olive color; *rare in this condition.*

212 1798 Cracked die, fine, good color.

213 1799 Very fine, sharp even impression, *obv.* and *rev.;* the best impression of this very rare cent we believe ever offered at public or private sale, smooth surface, dark color.

214 1800 Fine, red in color.

215 1801 $\frac{1}{100}$ Variety, very good.

216 1802 Fine, excellent impression.

217 1803 Uncirculated light olive.

218 1804 Copy in copper.

219 1805 Excellent impression, good color, *not fine.*

220 1806 Very good.

221 1807 Very good.

222 1808 Excellent impression, *not fine.*

223 1809 Strictly uncirculated, light olive color, very rare in this condition, *obv.* and *rev.* sharp and distinct.

224 1810 Excellent impression, *not fine.*

225 1811 Perfect die, fine sharp beautiful impression, *obv.* and *rev.; rare in this condition.*

226 1812 Very fine.

227 1813 Very fine, light olive color.

228 1814 Uncirculated, light olive color; *scarce in this condition.*

229 1816 Perfect die, very fine, light olive color.

230 1816 Uncirculated, broken die, bright red.

231 1817 Thirteen Stars, very fine, dark olive color, curl under bust distant from date.

232 1817 15 Stars, very fine sharp beautiful impression, dark olive color; *rare in this condition*

233 1817 Very fine, bright red.

234 1817 13 Stars, curl under bust, nearly touches date.

235 1818 Uncirculated, bright red.
236 1819 Large date, very fine red.
237 1820 Very fine, light olive color.
238 1820 Uncirculated, bright red, cracked die, extending around the stars.
239 1821 Sharp, beautiful proof, very slightly tarnished in color; *very rare in this condition.*
240 1822 Fine, light olive color, close date.
241 1822 Tarnished proof, slightly-rubbed, wide date.
242 1823 Over 22, very good, *scarce.*
243 1824 Fine distinct impression, dark color.
244 1825 Fine, light color.
245 1826 Very fine, light olive color.
246 1827 Dull proof, bright red.
247 1828 Very good.
248 1829 Uncirculated, sharp and beautiful impression, *obv.* and *rev.;* light olive color; *rare in this condition.*
249 1830 Fine, sharp impression.
250 1831 Uncirculated, bright red, proof surface.
251 1832 Very fine, dark olive.
252 1833 Very good.
253 1834 Dull proof, slightly rubbed, bright red.
254 1835 Very fine, light olive.
255 1836 Perfect die, very fine, light olive.
256 1837 Beautiful proof, bright red. *Rare in this condition.*
257 1838 Very fine, proof condition, dull impression.
258 1839 "1838 Head," uncirculated, bright red.
259 1839 "Booby Head," very fine, light olive.
260 1839 "1840 Head," very good.
261 1840 Large date, very fine, dark olive.
262 1840 Small date, tarnished date, sharp impression.
263 1841 *Obv.*, brilliant proof; *rev.*, tarnished proof.
264 1842 Very fine, good color.
265 1843 *Obv.*, brilliant proof; *rev.*, tarnished proof.
266 1844 *Obv.*, brilliant proof; *rev.*, tarnished proof.
267 1845 *Obv.*, proof; *rev.*, badly tarnished.
268 1846 Sharp and beautiful proof; *rare in this condition.*
269 1847 Uncirculated, beautiful olive color.
270 1848 *Obv.*, brilliant proof; *rev.*, tarnished proof.

271 1849 *Obv.*, brilliant proof; *rev.*, tarnished proof.
272 1850 *Obv.*, brilliant proof; *rev.*, tarnished proof.
273 1851 Uncirculated, beautiful olive color.
274 1852 *Obv.*, brilliant proof; *rev.*, tarnished proof.
275 1853 Uncirculated, red.
276 1853 Variety, uncirculated.
277 1854 Uncirculated, red.
278 1855 Straight date, bright red, uncirculated.
279 1855 Slanting date, uncirculated, bright red.
280 1856 Uncirculated, bright red.
281 1857 Large date, uncirculated, red.
282 1857 Large date, very fine.
283 1857 Small date, uncirculated, good color.

UNITED STATES HALF CENTS.

284 1794 Uncirculated, sharp and beautiful impression, dark olive color; *rare in this condition.*
285 1795 Thin Planchet, excellent condition, *not strictly fine.*
286 1803 Good sharp impression, *might be called fine.*
287 1804 Good sharp impression, *might be called fine.*
288 1805 Very fine, light olive color.
289 1809 Very good.
290 1811 Excellent impression, *not fine, scarce.*
291 1825 Very fine.
292 1828 13 Stars, very fine, proof surface.
293 1828 13 Stars, uncirculated, dark olive color.
294 1828 13 Stars, variety, uncirculated, light olive color.
295 1828 13 Stars, variety, uncirculated, light olive color.
296 1828 12 Stars, very fine, proof surface.
297 1829 Uncirculated, bright red.
298 1832 Proof, light olive, sharp impression; *rare in this condition.*
299 1832 Uncirculated, bright red.
300 1833 Uncirculated, tarnished proof, *rare.*
301 1833 Uncirculated, tarnished proof, *rare.*
302 1834 Very fine; *rev.*, proof surface, dark olive color.
303 1835 Uncirculated, tarnished proof.

304 1836 Beautiful proof, sharp impression, bright red, *excessively rare.*

305 1840 Brilliant proof, *very rare.*

306 1841 Brilliant proof, *very rare.*

307 1843 Brilliant proof, *very rare.*

308 1844 Tarnished proof, *very rare.*

309 1846 Tarnished proof, *very rare.*

310 1847 Tarnished proof, *excessively rare.*

311 1848 Tarnished proof, *very rare.*

312 1849 Small date, tarnished proof, *very rare.*

313 1850 Tarnished proof, dull impression, *scarce.*

314 1851 Tarnished proof, dull impression, *scarce.*

315 1851 Tarnished proof, very dull impression.

316 1852 Tarnished proof, *very rare.*

317 1854 Uncirculated, slightly tarnished.

318 1856 Proof surface, uncirculated, tarnished.

319 1857 Uncirculated, dark olive.

PATTERN PIECES.

320 1792 2 Experimental Cents, Silver Centre, Copies in Lead.

321 1792 4 Experimental Cents, Copies in Lead.

322 1838 Half Dollar, Silver; *obv.*, Goddess of Liberty seated; *rev.*, Flying Eagle, proof, *rare.*

323 1839 Silver Half Dollar; *obv.*, Bust of Liberty, surrounded by 13 Stars, date, 1839, under bust; *rev.*, Spread Eagle, with Shield, grasping three Arrows in the Left Talon, and Olive Branch in the Right Talon, surrounded by the Legend: "United States of America;" beneath the Eagle, "Half Dol." brilliant proof. The only specimen known, excepting the one in the Cabinet of the United States Mint, Phila.

324 1850 Silver Three-cent Piece, proof; *obv.*, Liberty Cap; *rev.*, III within a Wreath, dull proof.

325 1850 Ditto.

326 1851 Cent; *obv.*, Liberty seated; *rev.*, "1 Cent," within a wreath, struck in pure nickel, *rare.*

327 1853 Cent, struck in pure nickel, proof, *scarce.*

328 1856 Half Cent, struck in nickel, *very fine*, *scarce.*

329 1858 Large Eagle, Oak Wreath and Shield, Nickel Cent.
330 1858 Large Eagle, Oak Wreath without Shield, Nickel Cent.
331 1858 Large Eagle, Laurel Wreath, Nickel Cent.
332 1858 Large Eagle, Tobacco Wreath, Nickel Cent.
333 1858 Small Eagle, Oak Wreath with Shield, Nickel Cent.
334 1858 Small Eagle, Oak Wreath without Shield, Nickel Cent.
335 1858 Small Eagle, Laurel Wreath, Nickel Cent.
336 1858 Small Eagle, Tobacco Wreath, Nickel Cent.
337 1858 Indian Head, Oak Wreath with Shield, Nickel Cent.
338 1858 Eagle, Oak Wreath without Shield, Nickel Cent.
339 1858 Indian Head, Laurel Wreath, Nickel Cent.
340 1858 Indian Head, Tobacco Wreath, Nickel Cent.

341 1859 Silver Half Dollar; *obv.*, Head of Liberty; *rev.*, "Half Dollar," within a Wreath, proof, *scarce.*

342 1867 Five-cent Piece; *obv.*, Indian Head, surrounded by the Legend: "United States of America;" *rev.*, large V in centre of Shield, motto "In God we Trust" at the top, struck in aluminum, proof, *rare.*

343 1867 Five-cent Piece; *obv.*, Bust of Liberty, surrounded by Legend: "United States of America;" *rev.*, 5, the word "cents," in a curved line beneath the numeral, within a Laurel Wreath, motto "In God we Trust" at top, nickle, proof, *scarce.*

344 1868 Set of the Small Nickel Coinage, Five, Three and One-cent Patterns, proof, *scarce.*

345 1869 Set of the Small Nickle Coinage, Five, Three and One-cent Patterns, proof, *scarce.*

346 1869 Silver Twenty-five-cent Piece; *obv.*, Bust of Liberty; motto beneath, "In God We Trust," above, Legend: United States of America;" *rev.*, 25 within a Wreath, surrounded by the words "Standard Silver," *rare.*

346½ 1870 Silver Set, 9 pieces—3 Halves, 3 Quarters and 3 Dimes, brilliant proofs.

347 1850 Ring Cent, U. S. A., One-tenth Silver, *very fine*, *rare.*

UNITED STATES COINS.

348 1792 Half Disme; *obv.*, Bust of Martha Washington, Legend: "Lib., Par. of Science and Industry," date, under bust, 1792; *rev.*, Flying Eagle, beneath which "Half Disme," surrounded by the Legend: "United States of America," strictly uncirculated, beautiful impression, struck in copper, *extremely rare.*

349 1795 Silver Half Dime, sharp, beautiful impression, strictly uncirculated; *rare in this condition.*

350 1799 Silver Half Dollar, Six Stars facing, *very good.*

351 1799 Silver Half Dollar, Six Stars facing, *very good.*

352 1805 Silver dime, very fine impression, nearly uncirculated; *rare in this condition.*

353 1821 Silver Dime, uncirculated, *scarce.*

354 1823 Silver Dime, very sharp, fine impression, *scarce.*

355 1831 Silver Quarter, sharp, beautiful proof; *rare in this condition.*

356 1831 Silver Half Dime, uncirculated, *scarce.*

357 1832 Silver Dime, *fine.*

358 1871 Silver Half Dollar, brilliant proof.

359 1872 Silver Quarter, very fine proof surface.

360 1875 Twenty-cent Silver Piece, brilliant proof, *scarce.*

361 1875 Twenty-cent Silver Piece, brilliant proof, *scarce.*

362 1837 Silver Dime, without Stars, *fine.*

363 1875 Silver Dime, uncirculated.

AMERICAN GOLD COINS.

364 1860 Two-and-a-half-dollar Piece, brilliant proof, *scarce.*

365 1864 Three-dollar Piece, brilliant proof, *scarce.*

CALIFORNIA GOLD COINS.

366 1849 Five-dollar Gold Piece; *obv.*, 1849, surrounded by a Circle of Stars above the date, the letters N. G. and N. below the date; San Francisco in Exergue, "Full Weight of Half Eagle; *rev.*, Spread Eagle in Exergue, "California Gold without Alloy," *very fine.* One of the first pieces struck in California.

367 1852 Ten-dollar Piece; *obv.*, in four lines across the centre: "Augustus Humbert, United States Assayer of Gold, California, 1852," surrounded by very fine milling and lathe work; *rev.*, Spread Eagle and Shield, surrounded by Legend: "United States of America, Ten Dollars," 884 thous., *fine*, *rare.*

368 1854 One Dollar, round, *fine.*

369 1853 3 One Dollar, octagonal, *fine variety.*

370 1854 4 One Dollar, octagonal, *fine variety.*

371 1855 One Dollar, octagonal, *fine.*

372 1856 One Dollar, octagonal, *fine.*

373 1852 Half Dollar, round, *uncirculated.*

374 1853 4 Half Dollars, 2 round and 2 octagonal, *very fine.*

3 5 1854 3 Half Dollars, 1 round and 2 octagonal, *uncirculated.*

376 1871 Half Dollar, octagonal, *good.*

377 n. d. 4 Quarter Dollars, round, without date, *uncirculated.*

378 1853 Quarter Dollar, octagonal, *very fine.*

379 1859 Quarter Dollar, octagonal, *very fine.*

380 2 Specimens, virgin gold.

NORTH CAROLINA GOLD COINS.

381 n. d. Five-dollar Piece, C. Bechtler, 20 karat fine, 150 grains, Rutherford County, *very fine and scarce.*

382 1834 Five-dollar Piece, C. Bechtler, 20 karat fine, 140 grains, variety, *scarce.*

383 n. d. 2 One-dollar Pieces, Bechtler, 1 proof, 1 *fine.*

384 n. d. One-dollar Piece, C. Bechtler, *scarce, variety.*

PIKE'S PEAK COINS.

385 n. d Five dollar Gold Piece; *obv.*, Spread Eagle, surrounded by "Pikes Peak Gold Five D.;" *rev.*, Quartz Crushing Mill in centre, surrounded by "John Parson & Co., Oro," *very good, rare.*

386 1860 Two-and-a-half-dollar Gold Piece; *obv.*, Bust of Liberty, surrounded by Stars; *rev.*, Spread Eagle, surrounded by "Pike's Peak Gold, Denver, 2½ D.," *proof.*

387 n. d. Two-and-a-half-dollar Gold Piece, of J. J. Conway & Co., Bankers, *very fine, scarce.*

388 1860 2 Pieces, 20 Dollars and 10 Dollars, Clark, Gruber & Co., 1 Five-dollar Piece, Denver City Assay Office; are struck in copper, *very fine, scarce.*

UNITED STATES PROOF SETS.

389 1870 10 Pieces, brilliant proofs.

390 1873 10 Pieces, brilliant proofs.

391 1873 5 Pieces—1 Cent, Two Cents, Quarter, Ten Cents and Trade Dollar, brilliant proofs, *scarce in this condition.*

392 1873 Ditto.

393 1876 9 Pieces, brilliant proofs.

COLONIAL COINS, &c.

394 1652 Pine Tree Shilling, thin planchet; *obv*, very distinct impression; *rev.*, fair, *rare.*

395 1652 Pine Tree Shilling, small thick planchet; *obv.*, good; *rev.*, poor, *rare.*

396 1722 Rosa Americana Half Penny, uncrowned rose, *very good.*

397 n. d. Rosa Americana Penny, uncrowned rose, bright, *uncirculated, extremely rare.*

398 1723 Rosa Americana Penny, crowned rose, bright, *uncirculated, extremely rare.*

399 n. d. Rosa Americana Trial Piece, Penny struck on large planchet, uncrowned rose, size 24, American scale.

400 1767 Louisiana Penny, countermarked R. F., *very good, scarce.*

401 n. d. U. S. A. or Bar Cent, *very fine, rare.*

402 n. d. James II Tin Piece, original, *fine.*

403 1766 Pitt Token, no stamps, *very fine, rare.*

404 1776 Continental Currency, struck in tin, *very fine, very rare.*

405 n. d. 3 Columbia Tokens, all different, *scarce, very fine.*

406 1773 Virginia Cent, *fine, scarce.*

407 1760 Voce Populi, *fine, scarce.*

408 1781 North American Token, *very good, scarce.*
409 1787 Immunis Columbia, copper, doubtful, *very fine.*
410 1783 Nova Constellatio, U. S., *good, scarce.*
410½ 1785 Auctori Connec, *fine.*
411 1785 Auctori Connec, *very good.*
412 1786 Auctori Connec, *fine.*
413 1787 Franklin Cent, *very good, scarce.*
414 1787 New York Cent, *good, rare.*
415 1787 Massachusetts Cent, *very good, scarce.*
416 1786 3 Auctori Connec, varieties, *very good.*
417 1788 Auctori Connec, *very fine, scarce.*
418 Collection of Connecticut Cents, 1786 to 1788, consisting of 45 Pieces, all in excellent condition, and many varieties.
419 1788 Vermon Auctori, light olive color, *very fine, scarce.*
420 1788 Ditto, fine variety.
421 8 Pieces--Vermon Auctori, varieties, all in good condition.
422 n. d. Kentucky Cent, lettered edge, uncirculated, bright red, *very rare.*
423 n. d. Kentucky Cent, reeded edge, *very rare, fine.*
424 n. d. 2 Kentucky Cents, small and large planchets, *fine.*
425 1795 Talbot, Allum & Lee Cent, New York, lettered edge, bright and uncirculated.
426 1795 Ditto.
427 1796 2 Castorland Half Dollars, thick planchet, struck in copper, beautiful proofs.
428 1796 2 Ditto, thin planchets.

WASHINGTON PIECES.

(*Size by the American Scale of* 1-16*th.*)

429 Iron Shell—Very fine Bust of WASHINGTON, in excellent condition, history unknown. *Size* 64
430 Manly Medal; *obv.*, Bust of WASHINGTON, surrounded by the Legend: "Geo. Washington, Born in Virginia, February 11, 1732," in two lines beneath Bust; *rev.*, in nine lines, "General of the American Armies, 1775, Resigned 1783, President of the United States 1789," struck in lead, *very fine, rare.* *Size* 31

431 Manly Medal; *obv.*, Bust of WASHINGTON, surrounded by the Legend: "Geo. Washington, Natus Virginia, B. P., W. M. C.:" beneath the Bust in two lines: 11th of Feb., O. S., 1732;" *rev.*, same as No. 430, very fine copper bronzed, struck from Lincoln's dies, *fine*, *Size* 31

432 WASHINGTON before Boston, by Du Vivier, Original French Bronze Medal. *Size* 44

433 French Silver Shell—Bust of WASHINGTON on a Base, representing a Farmer Ploughing and Implements of Warfare; to the right, full-length Indian; to the left, the Goddess of Liberty; Legend: General George Washington, President of the United States; beneath the Base, in two lines: "Born February, 1732; died, December, 1799," proof. *Size* 42

434 1783 Washington Cent—Washington and Independence; *rev.*, United States, copper, *fine, scarce.*

435 1783 Washington Cent, same as No. 434, *fine.*

436 1783 Washington Cent, restrike, copper, proof.

437 1783 Washington Cent, Unity States of America, French Token, brass.

438 Washington Cent, Double Head, copper, *fine, scarce.*

439 Washington Cent—"GEORGIUS WASHINGTON," North Wales Token, copper, *very good.* *Size* 18

440 Washington Token: "Success to the United States," very fine brass, silvered, *scarce.* *Size* 18

441 Washington Penny: "Liberty and Security," thick die, copper, *very fine.* *Size* 21

442 1791 Washington Cent, very fine large Eagle, copper, dark olive color, *rare.*

443 1791 Washington Cent, small Eagle, copper, *very rare.*

444 1791 Washington Cent, fine large Eagle, copper, red.

445 1791 Washington Cent, fine small Eagle, good color, *very rare.*

446 1793 Liverpool Half Penny, with date under the Ship, copper, *very fine, rare.* *Size* 19

447 1793 Ditto, *fine.*

418 1793 Washington Medalette, by Wyon; *obv.*, Bust of WASHINGTON; Legend: "George Washington;" date beneath the Bust.; *rev.*, Emblems of Peace and War, surrounded by the circular line: "General of the American Armies, 1775; Resigned the Command 1783; Elected President of the United States 1789; Resigned the Presidency 1796." Motto on scroll in centre: "Repub. Amer.," copper, *very fine, rare.* *Size* 21

449 Conradt's Medal; *obv.*, Bust of Washington, with long Queue; beneath the Bust: "Conradt, 170 N. Fourth S.;" *rev.*, in six lines: "The Father of His Country, February 22d, 1832," in exerge, "Phila.," very good condition, struck in white metal, *extremely rare, and possibly unique.* *Size* 23

450 1797 Halliday's Medal, Commission Resigned, Presidency Relinquished, bronze, *very fine, rare.* *Size* 34

451 1797 Ditto. *Size* 26

452 1797 Mint Bronze Medal, "Presidency Relinquished, proof. *Size* 29

453 1797 Same, white metal, brilliant proof.

454 1797 Same, bronze, proof.

455 1797 Same, white metal.

456 1797 Same, white metal, proof, *rare.* *Size* 26

457 Same, bronze. *Size* 29

458 William Washington, Mint Medal, for Cowpens, bronze, proof. *Size* 29

459 Westwood Bronze Medal, Bust facing right; *rev.*, "With courage and fidelity he defended the rights of a free People; died December 14, 1799, aged 68;" above the lines thirteen long Arrows, fan shaped, *very fine, rare.* *Size* 26

460 Ditto, variety consisting of shorter Arrows, smaller Letters, and without period between the figures 68 in fact, differing from the others in small particulars generally. *Size* 26

461 Copper Gilt Medal, believed to be by Westwood; *obv.*, Bust of Washington, with close Periwig, with long Queue; Legend: "George Washington, O. B.: 14 December, 1799, Æ.: 68;" *rev.*, inscription in eight lines: "The Hero of Freedom, the pride of his Country and ornament of human nature, 1800," surrounded by a Wreath and the Legend: "Late President of the United States of America." *Size* 25

☞ This medal in silver brought $31 in the Mickley sale.

462 1818 English Shilling, countermarked with small Bust of Washington, cost Mr. Mickley £1 10s. in England, *fine, very rare.*

463 United States Cabinet Mint Medal, struck in silver, brilliant proof, *scarce.* *Size* 38

464 Same in bronze, brilliant proof.

465 Collection of large and small Speil Markes, in brass, all different, fifteen in number, *uncirculated.*

BRONZE PRESIDENTIAL MEDALS, (ALL PROOF.)

466	1797	John Adams, proof.	*Size* 32
467	1797	John Adams, proof, thinner planchet.	*Size* 32
468	1797	John Adams, proof.	*Size* 32
469	1797	John Adams, proof.	*Size* 32
470	1797	John Adams, proof.	*Size* 32
471	1801	Thos Jefferson, proof, *scarce.*	*Size* 64
472	1801	Thos. Jefferson, proof.	*Size* 48
473	1801	Thos. Jefferson, proof.	*Size* 32
474	1809	Jas. Madison, proof.	*Size* 48
475	1809	Jas. Madison, proof.	*Size* 40
476	1817	Jas. Monroe, proof.	*Size* 40
477	1817	Jas. Monroe, proof.	*Size* 32
478	1825	Jno. Q. Adams, proof.	*Size* 32
479	1829	Andrew Jackson, proof.	*Size* 40
480	1829	Andrew Jackson, proof.	*Size* 32
481	1837	Martin Van Buren, proof.	*Size* 48
482	1837	Martin Van Buren, proof.	*Size* 40
483	1837	Martin Van Buren, proof.	*Size* 32
484	1841	Jno. Tyler, proof.	*Size* 40

485 1841 Jno. Tyler, proof. *Size* 32

486 1845 Jas. K. Polk, proof. *Size* 32

486½ 1850 Millard Fillmore ; *rev.*, Plough, Flag, Farmer and Indian, &c., proof, *Size* 40

487 1853 Franklin Pierce ; *rev* , Plough, Flag, Farmer and Indian, proof. *Size* 40

488 1857 Jas. Buchanan ; *rev.*, Farmer, Indian, proof. *Size* 48

489 1862 Abraham Lincoln ; *rev.*, Farmer, Indians, &c., proof. *Size* 48

490 1862 Ditto. *Size* 40

491 1865 Andrew Johnson ; *rev* , Indian and Goddess of Liberty Clasping Hands in front of Monument, proof. *Size* 40

492 1869 U. S. Grant Inauguration Medal, proof. *Size* 32

U. S. BRONZE (PROOF) ARMY AND NAVY MEDALS.

493 General Ripley, for Battle of Chippewa ; *rev.*. Resolution of Congress, &c. *Size* 41

494 General Harrison, for Battle of Thames, *rev.*, Battle. *Size* 41

495 General Gaines, for Battle of Erie. *Size* 41

496 Commodore MacDonough, for Battle of Lake Champlain. *Size* 41

497 Capt. Jas. Biddle, for Capture of the Penguin. *Size* 41

498 Commodore Perry, for the Battle of Lake Erie, thick planchet. *Size* 41

499 General Jacob Brown, for the Battles of Chippewa. *Size* 41

500 General Morgan, for the Battle of Cowpens. *Size* 36

501 General Taylor, for the Battle of Monterey. *Size* 41

502 General Porter, for Battles of Chippewa. *Size* 41

503 General Gates, for Battle of Saratoga. *Size* 36

504 General Elliott, for Brave Conduct, &c. *Size* 41

505 Commodore Burrows, Memorial Medal—Enterprise and Boxer. *Size* 41

506 Commodore Lawrence, for Battle between Hornet and Peacock. *Size* 41

507 Commodore Decatur, for Battle between America and Macedonia. *Size* 41

508 Commodore Stewart, for Battle between Levant and Cyane. *Size* 41

509 Commodore Truxton, for Battle between the Constellation and La Vengeance. *Size* 36

510 General Rob. Henley Eagle, for Battle of Lake Champlain. *Size* 41

511 General Macomb, for Battle of Plattsburg. *Size* 41

512 General Jackson, for Battle of New Orleans. *Size* 41

513 General Blakeley, for Battle between Wasp and Reindeer. *Size* 41

514 General Winfield Scott, for the Battle of Chippewa. *Size* 41

515 Commodore Perry, for Battle of Lake Erie. *Size* 38

516 Commodore Perry ; *rev.*, Wreath containing the Letter "To," and blank field, "for Bravery at Lake Erie." *Size* 38

517 General Scott ; *obv.*, Bust, "Resolution of Congress," &c.; *rev.*, six interlocked Wreaths, containing representation of his various Battles during the Mexican War. *Size* 56

518 General Scott Testimonial Medal, from the State of Virginia. *Size* 57

519 General Taylor; *obv.*, Bust; *rev.*, Battle of Buena Vista, surrounded by two interlocked Rattlesnakes. *Size* 57

520 General Taylor, for the Battle of Palo Alto. *Size* 41

521 General Warrington, for Battle between the Peacock and Epervie. *Size* 41

522 Colonel Croghan, for the Battle of Sandusky. *Size* 41

523 General Jacob Jones, for the Battle between the Wasp and Frolic. *Size* 41

524 General Miller, for the Battle of Chippewa. *Size* 41

525 Commodore Bainbridge, for Battle between the Constitution and Java. *Size* 41

526 Commodore MacDonough, for the Battle of Lake Champlain. *Size* 41

527 John Paul Jones, for the Capture of the Serapis. *Size* 36

528 General Cassin, for the Battle of Ticonderoga. *Size* 41

529 General McCall, for the Battle between the Enterprise and Boxer. *Size* 41

530 Commodore Hull, for the Battle between the Constitution and Guerriere. *Size* 41

531 Commodore Perry, from the Merchants of Boston. *Size* 42

532 Governor Shelby, for Battle of the Thames. *Size* 41

533 John Egar Howard, for Battle of the Cowpens. *Size* 30

MISCELLANEOUS AMERICAN AND FOREIGN MEDALS.

534 Unique Silver Medal; *obv*, Bust of Jos. J. Mickley; beneath the Bust, date 1867; *rev.*, in 8 lines: "President of the Numismatic and Antiquarian Society of Philadelphia," brilliant proof.

☞This Medal, the only one of the kind struck in silver, was presented to Mr. J. J. Mickley, on January 2, 1868, by Messrs. Alfred B. Taylor, W. H. Key and C. Warner, committee; weight, 1040½ grains; value in silver, $2.70, in handsome velvet-lined case.

535 Jas. Ross Snowden, Director of the Mint; *obv.*, bust; *rev.*, U. S. Mint, bronze proof. *Size* 51

536 Robert M. Patterson, Director of the Mint; *rev.*, "Parting Token of Regard, from the Employees of the Mint." *Size* 41

537 Abraham Lincoln; *obv.*, Bust of Lincoln, surrounded by "Abraham Lincoln, President of the United States, born, died, &c.;" *rev.*, "With malice toward none, &c.!" Swedish Emancipation Medal, bronze proof, *rare.* *Size* 40

538 Shipwreck Medal, bronze proof. *Size* 42

539 Set 35 Bronze Medals, of the Kings and Queens of England, all different, inclosed in velvet-lined morocco case, with three velvet-lined countersunk trays; size, 9½ inches by 7½ inches, beautiful light olive color, *very fine.*

540 Set of 40 English and French Bronze Medals Commemorating Various Public Events, in velvet and silk-lined countersunk trays; size, 7½ inches by 9½ inches, beautiful olive color. All different. *Very fine.*

541 Jenny Lind Bronze Medal, struck at Stockholm; *obv.*, Bust of Jenny Lind; *rev.*, Monument, with Emblematic Figures, surrounded by Harps and Wreaths, in case, *rare.* *Size* 50

542 Bronze Proof Medal, by Pidgeon; *obv.*, Bust of Matthew Boulton; *rev.*, in four lines: "Inventus avt qui vitam excolvere per artis," surrounded by a wreath, inclosed in metallic case, *rare.* *Size* 40

☞ This medal cost Mr. Mickley £1 1s. in Europe.

543 Bronze Countersunk Medal, proof; *obv.*, Bust of Matthew Boulton, with inscription; *rev.*, a Variety of Mathematical Calculations, in metallic case. *Size* 26

544 White-metal Proof Medal; *obv.*, Bust of Queen Louise of Sweden and Norway; *rev.*, Figure of Victory, *scarce.* *Size* 28

544½ Same, in bronze, *scarce.*

545 Tin Impression Bust of Queen Victoria, unusually fine and very beautiful; present to Mr. Mickley by Mr. Wyon, medalist to the Queen, September 2, 1869.

546 Bronze Proof Medal: *obv*, Bust of King Charles XV, of Sweden and Norway; *rev.*, Steam Engine, Press, &c., *scarce.* *Size* 24

547 White-metal Proof Medal of the London International Exhibition, London, 1872, by Wyon, *scarce.* *Size* 19

548 White-metal Proof Lutheran Medal; *obv.*, Bust of Luther; *rev.* Seventh Jubilee, &c. *Size* 24

549 Silver Medal of the Martyrs on the Revocation of the Edict of Nantes; *obv.*, People devoured by Wild Animals; *rev.*, a Hanging Scene, and a Nude Woman being dragged at the Tail of a Horse, and various other Scenes of Martyrdom. *Size* 36

☞ This rare Medal was purchased by Mr. Mickley at the cost of £2 5s.

550 Bronze Medal—Pope Pius IX, by Voight; *obv.*, Bust; *rev.*, Virgin and Child, *scarce.* *Size* 30

551 Bronze Proof Medal—Pope PIUS IX.; *obv.*, Crowned Bust; *rev.*, the Œcumenical Council of Ten. *Size* 27

552 Prussian Numismatic Bronze Medal; *obv.*, Bust of Copernicus; *rev.*, "Born, Died, etc.," *scarce.* *Size* 26

553 German Numismatic Bronze Medal; *obv.*, Bust of Mozart; *rev.*, "Born, Died, etc.," *rare.* *Size* 26

554 Bronze Proof Medal; *obv.*, Bust of Bernardus Von Beskow; *rev.*, Allegorical Figures, History, Fame, &c, *scarce.* *Size* 35

555 Bronze Medal; *obv.*, Bust of Neimeyer; *rev.*, Allegorical Figures, *scarce.* *Size* 30

556 Bronze Medal of the Sangerfest; *obv.*, Figure of Music; *rev.*, View of Cologne, proof, *scarce.* *Size* 32

557 Bronze Medal—Germania Society, by Deschler, Ausburg; *rev.*, 5 Busts of Musical Celebrities in Medallion, proof, *scarce.* *Size* 29

558 Ditto in White Metal.

COINS OF ENGLAND, &c.

559 Set Charles II. Hammered Money, Four Pence, Three Pence, Two Pence and One Penny, silver, without date, *very fine*, *scarce.*

560 Ditto, 4 pieces, varieties, *very fine*, *rare.*

561 1675 Charles II Maunday Money—Four Pence, Three Pence, Two Pence and One Penny, *very fine*, *scarce.*

562 1687 James II Maunday Money—Four Pence, Three Pence, Two Pence and One Penny, *very fine*, *scarce.*

563 1694 William and Mary Maunday Money—Four Pence, Three Pence, Two Pence and One Penny, *fine*, *scarce.* The Penny pierced.

564 1699 William III Maunday Money—Four Pence, Three Pence, Two Pence and One Penny, *fine*, *scarce.*

565 1710 Anna Maunday Money—Four Pence, Three Pence, Two Pence and One Penny, *fine*, *scarce.*

566 1717 George I Maunday Money—Four Pence, Three Pence, Two Pence and One Penny, *fine*, *scarce.*

567 1746 George II Maunday Money—Four Pence, Three Pence, Two Pence and One Penny, *fine.*

568 1763 George III Maunday Money—Four Pence, Three Pence, Two Pence and One Penny, *fine.*

569 1792 George III Set Wire Money—Four Pence, Three Pence, Two Pence and One Penny, *uncirculated, rare.*

570 1800 George III Set Maunday Money—Four Pence, Three Pence, Two Pence and One Penny, proofs.

571 1818 George III Set Maunday Money—Four Pence, Three Pence, Two Pence and One Penny, Old Head, *variety scarce.*

572 1822. George IV Set Maunday Money—Four Pence, Three Pence, Two Pence and One Penny, proofs.

573 1786 George III, three sets, Maunday Money—12 pieces, *uncirculated.*

574 1787 3 George III Silver Pieces—One Shilling, 2 Sixpences, *uncirculated.*

575 1872 Set—Shilling, Six Pence and Three Pence, *uncirculated.*

576 1872 Set—Shilling, Six Pence and Three Pence, *uncirculated.*

577 1872 Set—Shilling, Six Pence and Three Pence, *uncirculated.*

578 1872 Set—Shilling, Six Pence and Three Pence, *uncirculated.*

☞ These four sets were obtained by Mr. Mickley at the British Mint.

579 1689 William and Mary Half Crown, *fine, scarce.*

580 1686 James II Crown, *very good, scarce.*

581 1809 Joseph Napoleon Spanish Dollar, *fine, scarce.*

582 1777 George III Pattern, £5 5s. piece, struck in white metal, gilt, *very fine, excessively rare.*

583 1871 Set Canada Silver Money—Fifty Cent, Twenty-five Cent and Ten-Cent Pieces, brilliant proofs.

584 1871 Ditto.

585 1862 Set Bronze Pieces, India—Half Anna, Quarter Anna, Half Piece, One-twelfth Anna, brilliant proofs, in velvet-lined morocco case, *rare.*

586 1862 Set 3 Pieces Bronze Coin, India Straits—One Cent, Half Cent, Quarter Cent, brilliant proof, in velvet-lined morocco case.

587 1872 Copper Penny and Half Penny, from the Birmingham Mint, *uncirculated.*

588 1863 Sarawak Cent and Half Cent, copper, brilliant proof, 2 pieces, *scarce.*

589 1863 Ditto, thinner planchet, 2 pieces.

590 1865 Hong Kong—One Mil, copper, 2 pieces, *uncirculated.*

591 1871 Prince Edward Island Cent, bronze, proof, *rare.*

592 1871 Ditto.

593 1872 Newfoundland Cent, bronze, *uncirculated, scarce.*

594 1872 Ditto.

595 1869–1872 Bronze Penny, Half Penny and two Farthings, *bright and uncirculated.*

COINS OF FRANCE.

596 1861 Silver Five-franc Piece—NAPOLEON III, *uncirculated.*

597 1857 Ditto, *uncirculated.*

598 1869 Silver Five-franc Piece—NAPOLEON III, *uncirculated.*

599 1870 Silver Five-franc Piece—Republic; *rev.*, Wreath without Legend, *very good, scarce.*

600 1870 Silver Five-franc Piece—Republic; *rev.*, Wreath; Legend. "Liberte, Egalite, Fraternitie," *uncirculated, scarce.*

601 1870 Ditto.

602 1871 Silver Five-franc Piece—Republic; *rev.*, one Male and two Female Figures, representing Liberty, Justice, &c., *uncirculated, scarce.*

603 1872 Ditto.

604 1872 Ditto.

605 1866 Silver Two-franc and One-franc Pieces—NAPOLEON III, *uncirculated.* 2 pieces.

606 1867 3 Silver Pieces—One Franc, Half Franc, and Quarter Franc, *very fine.*

607 1812 Half Franc of NAPOLEON BONAPARTE, *strictly uncirculated and rare in this condition.*

608 1831 Franc Piece—HENRY V, *very fine and rare.*

609 1852, 1853 and 1855 2 Half Francs, and Quarter Franc, proofs.

610 1869 2 Silver Two-franc Pieces, *uncirculated.*

611 1871 Silver Two-franc Piece—Republic; *rev.*, Wreath without Legend, *uncirculated, scarce.*

612 1871 2 Silver Two franc Pieces—Republic; *rev.*, Wreath with Legend, *uncirculated.*

613 1871 3 Silver Half-franc Pieces—Republic, with Legend, *uncirculated.*

614 1872 2 Silver Two-franc Pieces—Republic, *uncirculated.*

615 1872 2 Silver One-franc Piece—Republic, *uncirculated.*

616 1848 Centime—Republic, *uncirculated, scarce.*

617 1853 Set of Bronze Coins—NAPOLEON III, 5 pieces, *uncirculated.*

618 1853—1862 5 Bronze Coins—NAPOLEON III, *different varieties.*

619 1870 Caricature Bronze Medal of the Commune; *obv.*, Helmeted Bust of NAPOLEON III, Legend: "NAPOLEON III, Le Miserable, 2 Decembre;" *rev.*, a Spread Eagle with an Owl's Head, surrounded by Legend Vampire De La France, Sedan, 2 Septembre, 1870, *uncirculated, very rare.* *Size* 21

620 Ditto, *uncirculated.*

☞These two Medals were obtained by Mr. Mickley while in Paris, 1871.

621 1871 2 Bronze Coins—Ten Centimes and Five Centimes, Republic, *uncirculated.*

622 1872 2 Bronze Coins—Ten Centimes and One Centime, Republic, *uncirculated.*

623 1793 2 Pieces Gun Money—5 Sols, thick planchet, and 5 Sols, thin planchet. Siege of Mayence, *very fine, rare.*

624 6 Miscellaneous Copper Coins.

SPANISH COIN, &c.

625 1808 Thick Octagonal Silver Seige Piece—Stamped FERDINAND VII, 30s., struck in the Island of Minorca, *rare,* *Size* 23 by 20

626 8 Ancient Coppers, *various.*

627 Ten Interesting Copper Coins, struck in the Seventeenth Century, *fine, scarce, various.*

628 15 Ditto, struck in the Eighteenth Century, *very good, scarce.*

629 1868 Gold Coin, 10 Escudos, *uncirculated.*
630 1854 Gold Coin, 40 Reals, *very good.*
631 1845 Silver Coin, 1000 Reals, MARIA II., *fine.*
632 1860–64 2 Spanish Silver Half Dollars, 10 Reals, *fine.*
633 1867 2 Spanish Silver Dollars, ISABELLA II, *uncirculated.*
634 1870 3 Spanish Silver Dollars; *obv.*, Reclining Female Figure, representing Peace, *very fine, uncirculated.*
635 1868 Ditto, brilliant proof, *rare.*
636 1868 Ditto, brilliant proof, *rare.*
637 1871 4 Spanish Silver Dollars—AMADEUS I, *uncirculated.*
638 186?–'70 9 Spanish Silver Coins—One Peseta, size Twenty-Cent Piece, *various, very fine.*
639 1869–'70 9, Ditto, size Ten-cent Piece.
640 1870 Set Bronze Coins, 5 Pieces—Un Gramo, Dos Gramos, Cinco Gramos and Diez Gramos, with specimen planchet, 5 pieces, *uncirculated.*
641 1870 Ditto, 5 pieces, *uncirculated.*
642 1870 Ditto, 2 pieces, large and small bronze, *uncirculated.*
643 35 large and small Copper Coins, *mostly fine.*

COINS OF ITALY.

644 1848 2 Five-lire, silver, of Lombardy, *fine, scarce.*
645 1848 5-lire, silver, Republic of Venetia, *uncirculated, scarce.*
646 1870 2 Five-lire, silver, Victor Emanuel, *uncirculated, scarce.*
647 1871 Ditto.
648 1867 6 Silver Coins, VICTOR EMANUEL, size of Ten-cent Piece.
649 1866 Set Bronze Coins—VICTOR EMANUEL, One, Two, Five, and Ten-centismi, 4 pieces, *uncirculated.*
650 1866 Ditto, 4 pieces.
651 1867 Ditto, 4 pieces.
652 17 Bronze Coins—VICTOR EMANUEL, large and small, *uncirculated.*
653 1859 Set Bronze Coins, Tuscany—Five, Two, and One-centismi, *uncirculated.*
654 1859 Ditto.
655 1838 9 Silver Coins—FERDINAND II, size of Silver Dime, *uncirculated, scarce.*
656 1839 5 Ditto.

PAPAL COINS.

657 1839 Copper Coin—QUATTRINO GREGORY XVI, *uncirculated, rare.*

658 1848 Fifteen-Centisima di Lira Corente Copper Coin, plated, 2 pieces, *rare.*

659 1849 Set 4 Silver-plated Copper Coins—Republic Romana; has the Fasces with Axes and Liberty Caps; Forty, Sixteen, Eight and Four-baiocchi, *fine, rare.*

660 1850–'51 Set 4 Copper Coins, Pius IX—Two and One-and-one-half-baiocchi and One Quattrino, proof, *scarce.*

661 1857 Silver Coin, PIUS IX—Fifty-baiocchi, *uncirculated.*

662 1865 3 Silver Coins, PIUS IX—Twenty, Ten and Five-baiocchi, 2 proofs, the Twenty-baiocchi uncirculated.

663 1867 Silver Coin, PIUS IX—Five-lire, proof, *scarce, uncirculated.*

664 1867 2 Silver Coins, PIUS IX—One-lire and Five-soldi, *uncirculated, scarce.*

665 1867 2 Bronze Coins, PIUS IX—Two Soldi, proof.

666 1867 Set Bronze Coins, PIUS IX—One-Soldi, One-half-Soldi and One-Centessimo, *scarce.*

667 1868 2 Silver Coins, PIUS IX—Ten Soldi, *uncirculated.*

668 1869 2 Silver Coins, PIUS IX—Two-lire and One-lire, proof, *scarce.*

669 1869 2 Silver Coins, PIUS IX—One-lire and Ten-soldi, *uncirculated, scarce.*

670 1870 Silver Coin, PIUS IX—Five-lire, *uncirculated.*

GERMAN COINS.

BADEN.

671 1867–'69 2 Silver Coins—One and Half Gulden, *uncirculated, scarce.*

672 1870 Silver Coin—One Thaler, proof, *scarce.*

673 1870 Silver Coin—Three Kreuzer, 6 pieces, *uncirculated.*

674 1871 3 Copper Coins—2 One Kreuzers and one Half Kreuzer, *uncirculated.*

675 1871 2 Copper Coins—Half Kreuzer, *very fine.*

☞ Coined by Mr. Mickley at Carlsruhe.

PRUSSIA, ETC.

676 1870 Silver Coin—Two-thaler Piece, proof, *scarce.*

677 1870 Silver Coin—One Thaler, proof, *scarce.*

678 1866–'70 2 Silver Coins—One Thaler, *uncirculated.*

679 1870 7 Silver Coins—Two-and-half Silver Groschen, *uncirculated.*

680 1870 2 Coins—One Silver Groschen, *uncirculated*, and Half Silver Groschen, proof.

681 1870 Set Copper Coins—Four Pfenninge, Three Pfenninge, Two Pfenninge and One Pfenninge, *uncirculated.*

682 41 Small Copper and Bronze Coins, mostly Prussian, *some fine and uncirculated.*

682A 1876 Silver Coin, King William—One Thaler, *uncirculated.*

682B 1876 Ditto.

682C 1871 Ditto, proof.

682D 1871 Ditto, proof.

682E 1871 2 Coins—Two-and-a-half and One Silber Groschen, proof, *scarce.*

682F 1868 Half Silber Groschen, proof, *scarce.*

682G 1871 Four, Three and Two Pfenninge, copper, proof, *scarce.*

682H 1871 Three and One Pfenninge, copper, proof, *scarce.*

SAXONY.

683 1870 Silver Coin—One Thaler, John V; *obv.*, two Male Figures supporting Shield, *uncirculated, scarce.*

684 1871 Ditto; *obv.*, Equestrian Figure, *uncirculated.*

685 1871 Ditto, *uncirculated.*

686 1871 Ditto; *obv.*, Arms, Shield, &c., proof, *scarce.*

687 1869–'70 4 Small Silver Coins, *uncirculated.*

688 1869 3 Copper Coins—Five, Two and One Pfenninge, *uncirculated.*

FREE CITY OF FRANKFORT.

689 1848 Silver Coin—Two Thaler, *very good.*

690 1848 Silver Coin—Two Thaler; *obv.* and *rev.*, Eagle, *fine, scarce.*

691 1845 Silver Coin—Two Gulden, *fine.*

692 1860 2 Silver Coins—One Thaler, *uncirculated.*

693 1861 Silver Coin—Two Thaler, *very fine.*

694 1866 Silver Coin—Two Thaler, proof.

695 1862 One Thaler, silver, *fine, uncirculated.*

WURTEMBERG.

696 1848 One Thaler, silver, *fine, scarce.*

697 1869 Two Thaler, silver; *rev.*, Cathedral, brilliant proof, *scarce.*

698 1870 One Thaler, proof.

699 187 Half Gulden, proof.

700 1870–'71 11 Small Coins—One Kreuzer, silver, *uncirculated.*

701 1870 One-half Kreuzer, copper, *uncirculated.*

702 1870 One Thaler, proof.

703 1870 One-half Gulden, silver, proof.

704 1869 Two-and-a-half and One-quarter Kreuzer, copper, *uncirculated.*

BELGIUM.

705 1871 20 Francs Leopold II, gold, *very fine.*

706 1870 5 Francs Leopold II, silver, *very fine.*

707 1868–'9 Two and One Franc Pieces, silver, *very good.*

708 1869 2 Small Silver Coins, *uncirculated.*

709 9 Nickel and Copper Coins, small, *uncirculated.*

710 1849–'50 Set Copper Coins—Ten, Five, Two and One Centime, 4 pieces, *uncirculated.*

711 1847 Ditto, 4 pieces.

712 1860–'3 6 Nickel Coins, *uncirculated.*

713 8 Copper Coins, large and small.

FREE CITY OF BREMEN.

714 1863 One Thaler, proof.

715 1863 One Thaler, proof.

716 1864 Thirty-six Grote, proof.

717 1860 Twelve Grote, *uncirculated.*

718 1861 Six Grote, *uncirculated.*

719 1866 3 Copper Coins—Two-and-a-half Schwaren, *uncirculated.*

720 1859 3 Copper Coins—One Schwaren, *uncirculated.*

720½ 1847 Set Pattern Coins, Five Franc Pieces, silver, gold plated, 12 different varieties.

AUSTRIA.

721 1812 3 Pieces—Two and One Kreuzer and Fifteen Kreuzer, copper, *uncirculated.*

722 1818–'63 5 Copper Coins, various.

723 1790 One Kreuzer, *uncirculated, rare.*

724 1857 2 Pieces—One Thaler, *uncirculated.*

725 1869 4 Silver Half Thalers, Francis Joseph, *uncirculated.*

726 1780 Silver Dollar, Maria Theresa; fine Bust, with bare Head, sharp, *uncirculated, rare.*

727 1867 Two-thaler Piece, Francis Joseph, proof.

728 1871 One Thaler, proof.

729 1871 Half Thaler, proof.

730 1857 One Thaler, *very fine.*

731 1869, '70 and '71 3 Silver Coins, Hungarian; size, Half Dollar, *uncirculated.*

732 17 Silver Coins, from the size of Twenty-five Cents to Half Dimes, proofs, various, *uncirculated.*

733 1851 Set Coins—Three, Two, One, Half and Quarter Kreuzer, copper, brilliant proofs, 4 pieces.

734 1816 Set Coins—One, Half and Quarter Kreuzer, proofs, 3 pieces, *rarely found in this condition.*

735 1848 Two-kreuzer piece, thick planchet, proof, *scarce.*

736 1861 Four-kreuzer, thick planchet, copper, proof.

737 1858–'59 4 Small Copper Coins, *uncirculated.*

SWEDEN.

738 1738 Four-daler Piece, copper plate; size, 10 by 9 inches, ⅛ inch thick, *good condition.*

739 1732 Four-daler Piece, copper plate; size, 10 by 10½ inches, ⅛ inch thick, *fine.*

740 1743 Two-daler Piece, copper plate; size, 7½ by 8 inches, ⅛ inch thick.

741 1721 One-daler Piece, copper plate; size, 5½ by 5 inches, ⅛ inch thick.

742 1756 One-daler Piece, copper plate; size, 5 by 4 inches, ⅛ inch thick.

743 1720 Half-daler Piece, copper plate; size, 4 by 3½ inches, ⅛ inch thick.

744 1759 Half-daler Piece, copper plate; size, 4 by 3½ inches, ⅛ inch thick.

745 1735 Half-daler Piece, copper plate; size, 3½ by 3½ inches, ⅛ inch thick.

☞ 738 to 745, inclusive, are countermarked in the centre and on each corner; said to have been used in Sweden as currency, derived as taxes on the copper mines. All in good condition, *rare.*

746 1868 Gold Coin, Land. Shall., about $3 in value; *obv*, Bust of KING CHARLES XV; *rev.*, Arms, &c., proof.

747 1868 Gold Coin, 10 Francs: *obv.*, Bust of CHARLES XV, proof.

748 1869 Silver Crown, CHARLES XV, proof, *scarce.*

749 1870 Silver Crown, CHARLES XV, proof, *scarce.*

750 1871 Half and one-third Crown, 25 Ore and 10 Ore, CHARLES XV, proof, *scarce*, 4 pieces.

751 1864 2 Pieces Silver, one-third Crown, *very fine.*

752 1862 3 Silver Coins, 50 Ore, proof.

753 10 Small Silver Swedish Coins, from 50 Ore to 10 Ore, various dates, *uncirculated.*

754 1715–'19 15 Copper Dalers, Charles XII; *obv.*, Figure of Time; *rev.*, One Daler, different varieties, *fine.*

755 1867 2 Five Ore Copper Pieces, Charles XV, *uncirculated.*

756 1871–'2 2 Ore Copper Pieces, proofs.

757 17 Small Copper and Bronze Coins, Charles XV, *uncirculated.*

758 1875–'76 2 Silver Pieces, Oscar II—One Krone and Ten Ore.

759 1876 4 Copper Coins—2 Five Ore, 1 Two Ore and 1 One Ore, varieties, *uncirculated, scarce.*

760 1873 Silver Piece—One-third Crown, proof.

761 1873 Silver Piece—One-third Crown, proof.

MISCELLANEOUS FOREIGN COINS AND MEDALS.

762 1871 Five-thousand Reis Gold Coin, Portugal, proof.

763 1871 Two-thousand Reis Gold Coin, Portugal, proof.

764 1855 One Thousand Reis Gold Coin, Portugal, proof.

765 1862 Gold Sovereign, Queen Victoria, *uncirculated.*

766 1872 Gold Sovereign, Queen Victoria, St. George and the Dragon, *very fine.*

767 1872 Half Gold Sovereign, Queen Victoria, *very fine.*

768 1870 Gold Sovereign, Australia, Sydney Mint, *fine, scarce.*

769 1864 Gold Half Sovereign, Australia, Sydney Mint, *very fine, scarce.*

770 1 Complete Set Bronze Coins, Tunis, Modern, 6 pieces, from the size of a Dollar to Half Dime, proof.

771 Ditto.

772 1808 Fifty S's.—NAP. LODEW I, of Holland, in silver box, cut from an old German crown, *very fine.*

773 Bavarian Silver Dollar—LOUIS II; *rev.*, Patron Saint of Bavaria, by Voigt, proof, *scarce.*

774 2 Bronze Turkish Coins, (Tunis), proofs; size half dollar.

775 Silver Crown—Free City of Frankfort, proof.

776 Religious Commemoration Silver Medal—Free City of Frankfort, proof. *Size* 23

777 1848 Silver Constitutional Medal—Free City of Frankfort, *fine.* *Size* 23

778 1862 Schutzenfeste Silver Medal—Free City of Frankfort, *very fine.* *Size* 21

779 1861 Silver Thaler—Bust of WILLIAM and AUGUSTA, of Prussia, *uncirculated.*

780 1849 Two-and-a-half G., Silver—WILLIAM III, Netherlands, proof.

781 1860 Two-and-a-half G. and Half G., proof, 2 pieces.

782 1858 Ditto, *uncirculated.*

783 1863 4 Silver Coins—2 One G., Half G. and Ten Cent, 2 proofs and 2 uncirculated.

784 1849–1855 7 Small Silver Coins—2 uncirculated, 5 proofs, *different varieties.*

785 1857 Set 3 Bronze Coins—Two-and-a-half, One and Half Cent, Netherlands, *uncirculated.*

786 1857 Ditto.

787 13 Small Copper Coins—Netherlands, *uncirculated.*

788 7 Hungarian Silver Coins—from the size of Two G. to One Kreuzer, modern, *uncirculated.*

789 1868 3 Bronze Coins—Hungarian, Four Kreuzer, *uncirculated, scarce.*

790 Prussian Medal—Battle of the Prague, 6th May, 1757, brass, *fine.* *Size* 24

791 1623 Swedish Hammered Silver Crown—FREDERICK, Duke of Brunswick, *fine, rare.*

792 1866 Silver Thaler—King of Prussia, *fine.*

793 1869 Spanish Silver Coin—Two Peseta, *fine.*

794 1867 Bavarian Silver Dollar—LOUIS II, by Voight; *rev.*, Patron Saint, proof, *rare.*

795 1842 Silver Thaler of Hanover, *fine.*

796 3 Japanese Coins—2 Oval and 1 Round, brass, *fine.*

797 4 Silver Coins—Russian, German and Hungarian, size from Fifty to Twenty Cent Pieces, *fine.*

798 39 Small Foreign Silver Coins, from the size of Half Dime to Twenty Cent Piece, various dates, *fine.*

799 Turkish Silver Dollar, modern, *good.*

800 30 Large and Small Silver Coins, mostly Maunday Money, some duplicates, *all in fine condition.*

801 1869 5 Greek Coins, bronze, large and small, *uncirculated.*

802 11 Large and Small Turkish Coins, copper, varieties.

803 2 Small Egyptian Gold Coins, *very fine.*

804 2 Small Turkish Copper Coins, proof.

805 26 Large and Small Bronze Coins of Romania and Greece, some duplicates, *uncirculated.*

806 1867 Bronze Coins of Sweden—2 Two Ore and 4 One Ore, 6 Pieces, duplicates.

807 1866, '68 & '69 Thaler, One Gulden, One-half Gulden, Six Kreuzer, Three Kreuzer, One Kreuzer, of Bavaria—Louis II, proofs.

808 1866 Silver Thaler—Louis II, Bavaria, *fine.*

809 5 Small Silver Coins, of Bavaria, *fine.*

810 2 Small Bronze Coins, of Bavaria, proofs.

811 1868 4 Hungarian Kreuzers, bronze, *uncirculated.*

812 1868 Set Danish Silver Coins—Christianus VII, Two Rigsdaler, One Rigsdaler, One-half Rigsdaler, Sixteen Skilling and Four Skilling, 5 pieces, *uncirculated, scarce.*

813 1863 Danish Two Rigsdaler; *obv.*, Christianus VII; *rev.*, Frederick II, *uncirculated, rare.*

814 1854–'58 4 Danish Silver Coins—Christianus VII, Rigsdaler, Sixteen Skilling and Four Skilling, *uncirculated.*

815 1862 Twenty and Ten-cent Silver Pieces, Danish West Indies—Frederick VII: *rev.*, Barque, &c., proofs, 2 pieces.

816 6 Small Danish Silver Coins, various dates, *good.*

817 8 Danish Bronze Coins—6 One Skilling and 2 Half Skilling, *uncirculated.*

818 1868 1 Silver Greek Coin, size of Half Dollar, *uncirculated.*

819 1869 4 Greek Bronze Coins—Ten Lepta to One Lepta, *uncirculated.*

820 1868 Set Greek Bronze Coins—Ten, Five and One Hofa, 3 pieces, *uncirculated.*

821 1868 Ditto.

822 1868 Ditto.

823 1870 Silver Coin of Romania—One Leu, *uncirculated.*

824 1867 Set Romania Bronze Coins—Ten, Five, Two and One Bani, *uncirculated, scarce.*

825 1848 Danish Silver Dollar; *obv.*, CHRISTIAN VIII; *rev.*, FREDERICK II, *very good, scarce.*

826 1872 Set Coins of Equador—Two and One Centavo, 2 pieces, *uncirculated, scarce.*

827 1872 Cent, copper, Newfoundland, *scarce.*

828 1871 One Cent, Prince Edward's Island, bronze, *uncirculated.*

829 2 Metz and Sedan Medals, 1870—Bust of PRINCE ALBERT and PRINCE GEORGE, of Saxony, gold and silver plated, proof. *Size* 13

830 1782 Silver Peace Medal—Holland; *obv.*, 1 Male and 2 Female Figures; *rev.*, Hand, with the Arms of Holland Protruding from the Clouds, proof, *rare.* *Size* 28

831 1847–'70 Bronze Coin of Portugal—XX, X, V, III, II, I Milreis, 6 pieces, *fine.*

832 1865–'68 Ditto—XX. X, V, III Milreis, 4 pieces.

833 18 5–'68 Ditto—XX, X, V, XII Milreis, 4 pieces.

834 19 Large and small Bronze and Copper Coins of Portugal and Brazil, varieties, *all in good condition.*

835 Oval Medallion in Wedgewood of BENJAMIN FRANKLIN, *very fine, in the most perfect condition.*

☞Purchased by Mr. Mickley in England for £1 1s.

836 1870 Silver Thaler of Saxony, proof.

837 1590 3 Copper Coins, struck at Geneva, Switzerland, *very fine, very rare.*

☞This set cost Mr. Mickley $5 in Switzerland.

838 1870 Silver Thaler—Mecklenburg, proof.

839 1864 Silver Thaler—Hanover, GEORGE V, *very good, scarce.*

840 1871 Silver Thaler—Free State of Bremen, *uncirculated, scarce.*

841 1864 Silver Thaler—Bremen, (Handel Medalt,) proof.

842 1863 Silver Thaler—(Jubilee), Free State of Bremen, dull proof.

843 1864 Silver Coin—Free State of Bremen, 20 Grote, *uncirculated.*

844 Canadian Marriage Medal; *obv.*, Hand Clasping a Torch, surrounded by "William Dummer Powell and Ann Murray, intermarried 3rd October, 1775;" *rev*, 8 lines within a Wreath, viz.: "To Celebrate the Fiftieth Anniversary, Upper Canada, 3rd October, 1825," fine copper, *very rare.* *Size* 24

845 1871 Set Portuguese Silver Coins—500, 200, 100 and 50 Reis, *uncirculated.*

846 1868 4 Bronze Coins of Portugal, Duplicates, *uncirculated.*

847 1851 Five-franc Piece, silver—Helvetia, Switzerland, *very fine, scarce.*

848 1850 Two and One-franc Pieces, silver—Helvetia, Switzerland, *very fine, scarce.*

849 1861 Three, Two and One-franc Silver Pieces—Helvetia, Switzerland, *fine.*

850 1850 One-franc and 3 Half Franc, silver—Helvetia, Switzerland, *very fine.*

851 15 Small Brass and Copper Coins of Helvetia, various dates and varieties, *uncirculated.*

852 1870 Silver Thaler—Darmstadt, *very fine, uncirculated.*

853 1871 2 Silver Coins—1 Kreuzer, *fine.*

854 1871 5 Bronze Coins—1 Pfennig, *uncirculated.*

855 1867 4 Bronze Coins of Romania—10, 5, 2 and 1 Bani, (the 10 Bani, proof), *uncirculated.*

856 1867 Ditto.

857 1867 4 Bronze Trial Pieces; *obv.*, Arms; *rev.*, Blank.

858 1870 Set Bronze Coins, Paraguay—Four, Two, and One Centesimo, 3 pieces, *uncirculated, scarce.*

859 1870 Ditto, 3 pieces.

860 1871 2 Nickle Coins—One Penny, Half Penny, of Jamaica, *uncirculated.*

861 1870 10 Small Bronze Coins, of Helvetia, Switzerland, duplicates, *all uncirculated.*

862 1863 Set Bronze Coins, Hayti—Twenty, Ten and Five Centimes, 3 pieces, proof, *scarce.*

863 1863 Ditto, 3 pieces, *scarce.*

864 1741 Admiral Vernon Medal—Capture of Carthagena, brass *very fine, rare.* *Size* 24

865 1741 Ditto, fine variety, *rare.*

866 1793 Medal struck in Iron—PETER WARGENTIN, German, *rare.* *Size* 22

867 Admiral Vernon Medal—Porto Bello, brass, *very fine, rare.*

868 2 Coins, 1 silver and 1 copper—PHILIP II, of Spain, *rare, very good.*

869 7 Roman Coins, from the Greek Mint at Alexandria, small, brass, fine varieties.

870 13 Ancient Silver Coins—(Becker's counterfeits), *scarce.*

871 Silver Penny of Sweden, Eric, *fair, rare.*

872 9 Silver Shells—Bracteates of Magdeburg, of the 12th Century, from size of Silver Dollar to Quarter Dollar, *very rare fine condition.*

873 Ancient Silver Coin—KING RODOLFOS, believed to be one of Becker's counterfeits.

874 Roman Coin, brass, PHILIP, the Arabian, *scarce.*

875 Large Brass Coin—DIOCLETIAN, *scarce.*

876 Roman Aes, reduced, *very good and rare.*

877 Second, Brass—TIBERIUS, *fine, rare.*

878 Ditto, variety, *good.*

879 Roman Coin, struck at the Greek Mint at Alexandria, *scarce.*

880 Roman Coin—GALLIENUS, small, brass, *fine, scarce.*

881 Roman Coin, small, brass, *Posthumos, good, scarce.*

882 Roman Coin—Second Bronze of FAUSTINA, *fair, scarce.*

883 Greek Coin—HIERO, of Sicily, small, brass, *very good, rare.*

884 Lot Ancient Coins, found at the Ruins of Pompeii, about 25, *very poor.*

885 Roman Coin—CONSTANTINE, the Great, small, brass, *fair, scarce.*

886 Silver Coin—SEBASTIAN I, of Portugal, size of a Dime.

887 1870 Bronze Coin—Republic of Spain, Two Gramos, *uncirculated.*

888 Exposition Medal, Granada, lead, *very fine.* *Size* 19

889 Crystal Palace White Metal, Exhibition, Portugal, pierced, proof. *Size* 23

890 1872 2 Silver Coins of Sweden—Ten Ore, proofs, duplicate.

891 100 Copper, Bronze, Nickel, Brass Coins, Medalettes, Tokens, Foreign and American. A Splendid Collection of Fine and Good Pieces, some quite interesting and scarce.

892 Ancient Roman Coin, Colony of Nismes—AUGUSTUS and AGRIPPA, brass, *very fine.*

893 Ancient Roman Coin, of CONSTANTINE, small, brass, *fine.*

894 1828 French Louis D'Or, gold, *very fine.*

895 1848 1 "Species;" *obv.*, Bust of FREDERICK VII, King of Denmark; *rev.*, CHRISTIAN VIII, *uncirculated, scarce.*

896 1853 1 "Species;" *obv.*, Bust of FREDERICK VII; *rev.*, Arms Denmark, *uncirculated.*

897 1854 2 Rigsdaler; *obv.*, Bust of FREDERICK VII; *rev.*, Wreath, *uncirculated.*

898 1851 1 Rigs Bank Daler; *obv.*, Bust of FREDERICK VII; *rev.*, Arms of Denmark, *uncirculated.*

899 1842 32 Rigs Bank Skilling, Denmark, *fine.*

900 2 Danish Silver Coins—Two-thirds Rigsdaler, 179 , and Twenty-skilling Piece, Schl. Holst., 1789, *very good.*

901 2 Danish Silver Coins—Two-thirds Rigsdaler, 1830, and Half Rigs Bank Daler, 1839, *very good.*

902 11 German Base Coins, size of Half Dime to size of Silver Quarter.

903 3 Danish Copper Coins, thick planchet, *very fine.*

904 French Brass-plate Medal; *obv.*, Male Bust.

UNITED STATES STEEL DIES, HUBS, &c.

905 1784 Hub—WILSON PEALE; *obv.*, Bust of Peale, slightly damaged, *unique.*

906 1799 2 Hubs; *obv.* and *rev.* of Washington Medal, Presidency Relinquished, *very fine condition.*

907 1797 1 Hub—JOHN ADAMS, Mint Medal.

908 1796 1 Hub—Letter Foundry of Philadelphia, Established 1796, Figure of Industry, etc., *fine.*

909 1806 Hub; *obv.*, United States Dime, *very good.*

910 1806 Hub; *obv.*, United States Silver Twenty-five Cent Piece, *good.*

911 1807 Hub; *obv.*, Half Eagle, *good.*

912 1811 2 Hubs; *obv.* and *rev*, United States Half Cent; *rev.* slightly damaged on edge.

913 1816 2 Hubs; *obv.* and *rev.* United States Cent, *fair condition.*

914 1817 2 Hubs; *obv.*, and *rev.* United States Cent, *good condition.*

915 1820 1 Hub; *obv.*, Half Eagle, *good.*

916 1 Hub; *rev.*, United States Twenty-five Cent Piece, about 1820.

917 Miscellaneous Lot Dies and Hubs; *obvs.* and *revs.* of American Coins, 8 pieces, *broken, and in poor condition.*

918 2 Hubs—Jackson Inauguration Medal; *obv.* and *rev.* *very fine.*

COLONIAL, CONTINENTAL, CONFEDERATE AND UNITED STATES PAPER MONEY, &c.

919 110 Notes—Colonial Paper Money, Pennsylvania, from Three Pence to Fifty Shillings, some duplicates, containing a number of very Scarce Notes, *generally good condition.*

920 88 Ditto, from Three Pence to £4, some duplicates, containing a number of Scarce Notes, *generally in good condition.*

921 109 Notes—Colonial Paper Money, Maryland, from Smallest to Largest Denominations, containing a number of Scarce Notes, some duplicates, *very fair.*

922 44 Ditto, some scarce, some duplicate, *poor.*

923 43 Ditto, from One-Ninth Dollar to Eight Dollars, few duplicates, some scarce, *in fair to good condition.*

924 50 Notes—Red and Black Issue, New Jersey Colonial Money, One Shilling to £6, some scarce, but few duplicate, *good.*

925 Complete Set Delaware Paper Money, January 1st, 1776—One, One-and-a-half, Two-and-a-half, Four, Five, Six, Twenty Shilling, *scarce as a set, good condition.*

926 15 Notes—Delaware Paper Money; this Lot includes a Complete Set of January 1st, 1776, *fair condition.*

927 1 Sheet—Containing 4 Notes of New Jersey, £3 each, March 25th, 1776, *uncirculated.*

928 2 New Jersey Colonial Notes, April 23d, 1761, and May 1st, 1758, £6 each, red issue, *good condition, scarce.*

929 34 Notes, State of Massachusetts Bay—One to Twenty Dollars, *fine, pierced or canceled.*

930 4 Notes, State of Massachusetts Bay—One Dollar, 1770, *fine.*

931 11 Small Notes—Massachusetts State; *rev.*, Pine Tree, from One Shilling, Sixpence, to Five Shilling, Sixpence, *pierced, good, scarce.*

932 10 Notes—State of Massachusetts Bay, 1 to 20 Dollars, all different pierced, *uncirculated, scarce.*

933 7 Notes—State of Rhode Island and Providence Plantations, 1 to 7 Dollars, all different, *good, scarce.*

934 9 Notes—State of Connecticut, from 2d to 40s., all different pierced, *scarce, good.*

935 8 Notes—State of New Hampshire, from 1 to 20 Dollars, pierced, *fair condition, rare.*

936 14 Notes—Virginia, 1 to 100 Dollars, *fair condition, rare, few duplicates.*

937 2 Notes—State of North Carolina, August 8, 1778, 5 to 10 Dollars, *good, rare.*

938 1 Note—Georgia, 5 Dollars, 1777, Seal, Cannon, &c., in Blue Ink, red issue, *very fine, rare.*

939 1 Note—Georgia, 1777, Seal, Snake in Green Ink, red issue, *fair condition rare.*

940 4 Notes—New York Water Works, 2, 4 and 8 Shillings, August 2, 1775, *good, rare.*

941 3 Notes—Colony of New York, 1771, February 16, 10s., £1 and £5, *good, rare.*

942 1 Note—State of New York, April 18, 1786, £1, *poor, rare.*

943 Lot 6 Notes—Colonial and Continental, *various, good.*

944 5: Notes—Continental Congress, issues from 1 to 60 Dollars, *arranged, good condition.*

945 32 Notes—Continental, from 1 to 6 Dollars to 60 Dollars, all good, duplicate, *fine, scarce.*

946 4 Notes—Bank of North America, 1 Penny Each. August 6, 1789, *uncirculated, rare.*

947 1 Note—Bank North America, Three Pence, August 6, 1789 : *rev.*, colored, *uncirculated, rare.*

948 1 Engraved Copper Plate of $10—Continental Currency, September 26, 1778, Seal Confederatio, *unique, fine condition.*

949 1 Sheet Containing 16 Notes—(2 Sets) Pennsylvania Colonial Money, from 1 Shilling to Half Crown, April 25, 1776, *uncirculated.*

950 Ditto—Variety in signatures.

951 Ditto—1 set 8 notes, *uncirculated.*

952 1 Dollar Note—Hungarian Lurd, February 2, 1852, L. Kossuth, *fine.*

953 6 Foreign Bank Notes, &c., various.

954 Lottery Ticket—Patterson, N. J., Prior to the Revolution, *fine.*

955 Lottery Ticket—"Conestogoe Bridge." 1761, signed Joseph Simon, *fine.*

956 Lottery Ticket—St Peters' Church, 1765, signed Henry Harrison, *fine.*

957 St. Catherine Toll Bridge—25 Cent Note, Louisiana, September 15, 1816, *fair.*

958 Humbug Glory Bank—6 Cent Shinplaster, 1837.

959 Ditto—5 Cent Shinplaster, 1834.

960 Bank Coffee House—"Back of the United States Bank," 6¼ Cent Shinplaster, no date, (about 1837.)

961 State of North Carolina—One-dollar Note, October, 1861, *good.*

962 1 Sheet—Set Notes, "City of Trenton, N. J.," Five to Fifty Cents, uncut, signed.

963 Virginia Treasury Notes—One Dollar, July, 1862.

964 Five Confederate Notes—One, Five, Ten, Fifty and One Hundred Dollars.

965 78 Old Local Notes, Checks, &c, some rare and interesting.

966 Colonial Note—North Carolina, 1754, Eight Pence; Seal: Bear, *poor condition, very rare.*

967 Colonial Note, North Carolina—Twenty Shillings, 1748; Seal: Cap of Mercury, *fair, very rare.*

968 Colonial Note, Province of North Carolina—£3, 1771; Seal: Magna Charta, *good, rare.*

969 North Carolina—Ten Shillings, Proclamation Money, 1761, *fine, rare.*

970 110 Old Local Notes, Shinplasters, Bank Notes, &c., *good.*

971 22 Foreign Bank Notes, different.

972 Frame, containing 4 Notes, (3 Checks and 1 Shinplaster,) checks signed Lewis M. Lane, Daniel Webster and Lewis Cass.

973 Portrait of GEORGE CALVERT, the First Lord of Baltimore, in gilt frame.

☞ This old frame was the original property of Squire Gough, of Hartford county, Maryland, a relative of Charles Carroll, of Carrollton. Rare.

974 Frame, with Old MSS., entitled "Union List of 1771:" Hugh Roberts, Benjamin Franklin, Samuel Neave, Samuel Morris, Luke Morris, Samuel Preston Moore, Joseph Stretch, William Fishbourn, Rich. Hockley, Israel Pemberton, Philip Benezett, Isaac Paschall, Thomas Wharton, Joshua Howell, Joseph Wharton, Jr., Samuel Purviance, Samuel Hudson, Mr. Wishart, Samuel Powell, Thomas Foxcroft, Enoch Story, Charles Moore, Joseph Pemberton, Peter Stretch.

975 2 Sheets Copper, electrotype, of *obv.* and *rev.* of Confederatio Coin, 1785.

976 Horn Seal, 1757—ISAAC MANN, Doctor of Divinity, Dublin.

977 1 Nickle American Scale for Measurement of Medals and Coins.

978 1 Brass Sliding Scale, containing American and French Scale for the Measurement of Medals and Coins.

979 1 Numismatist's Large Magnifying Glass, with handle.

980 1 Small ditto, folding.

981 Box, containing Pair Gold Scales and Set of Weights.

982 Medal Box, Morocco, 8 by 12 inches.

983 2 Electrotype Plates, showing the gold, silver and copper coinage of the United States, date and variety of each coin, 1793 to 1858, *good condition.*

NUMISMATIC WORKS.

984 15 Pamphlets—Dates and Rarity of the United States Coins, by J. J. Mickley.

985 Cogan's MSS.—Priced Catalogue of Foote's Sale, March 1859.

986 Thomas & Sons' Priced Catalogue Kline Sale, 1855, *rare.*

987 Ditto, not priced.

988 Lot 93—Miscellaneous, Foreign and American Coins Catalogue, &c.

989 4 Sotheby & Wilkinson's Priced Catalogue for 1861, all different.

990 6 Ditto, 1862, no duplicates.

991 9 Ditto, 1863, do

992 9 Ditto, 1865, do

993 12 Ditto, 1866, do

994 9 Ditto, 1867, do

995 9 Ditto, 1868, do

996 11 Ditto, 1869, do

997 8 Ditto, 1870, do

998 6 Ditto, 1871, do

999 10 Ditto, 1872, do

1000 7 Ditto, 1873, do

1001 9 Ditto, 1874, do

1002 7 Ditto, various dates.

1003 84 Ditto, unpriced, various dates.

1004 27 Foreign, unpriced catalogues, various.

1005 19 Foreign, Catalogues, some priced.

1006 40 American and Foreign Catalogues, some with Photographic Plates.

1007 34 American Catalogues.

1008 38 American Catalogues.

1009 Trésor de Numismatique et de Glyptique ou Recueil Général de Médailles, Monnaies, Pierres Gravées, Bas-reliefs, &c., tant Anciens que Modern esles plus Interessants sous le Rapport de L'Art et de L'Histoire. Graves par les Procédés de M. Achille Collas sous la Direction de M. Paul Delaroche, de M. Henriquel Dupont et de M. Charles Lenormant—Medals of Germany, 1 vol; Medals of Italy, 2 vols.; Medals of the Popes, 1 vol.; Medals of France, 5 vols.; Modern Money, 1 vol.; Bas-reliefs, 3 vols.; Medals, etc., of the Roman Emperors, 1 vol.; Coins of Greece, 1 vol.; Gallery of Mythology, 1 vol.; Seals of England, 1 vol., and Seals of France, 3 vols. illustrated with numerous fine steel engravings, executed in the highest grade of art, 20 vols., folio, half morocco, gilt tops. Paris, n.d.

☞ This work cost Mr. Mickl y over $500, and is one of the best and most elaborate works ever published on this subject.

1010 Folkes. Martin—Table of English Silver Coins from the Norman Conquest to the Present Time, with their Weights, Intrinsic Values and some Remarks upon Several Pieces, folio, large paper, uncut. London, 1745.

1011 A Series of Medals, representing all the Remarkable Events, from the Revolution to the Death of King George I, folio, half bound. London, 17—

1012 Cardonnel, Adam de—Numismata, Scotiae; or, a Series of the Scottish Coinage, from the Reign of William the Lion to the Union, numerous plates, 4to, half morocco. Edinburgh, 1786

1013 Sharp. Thomas—Catalogue of Provincial Copper Coins, Tokens, Tickets and Medalettes issued in Great Britain, Ireland and the Colonies during the Eighteenth and Nineteenth Centuries, arranged according to Counties, &c., with particulars of their Fabrication, Names of Artists, and Miscellaneous Remarks, illustrative of the Rarity of Particular Specimens, described from the originals in the collection of Sir George Chetwynd, 4to, half morocco, uncut. London, 1834

☞ Presentation Copy, with Autograph Letter, signed by Sir George Chetwynd.

1014 Snelling on the Coins of Great Britain, France and Ireland, illustrated with 71 copper plates, 4to, half calf. London, 1762

1015 Lot Engravings—Coins of England.

1016 Lot Engravings—Coins of the Bible.

1017 Lindsay. John—View of the Coinage of Ireland from the invasion of the Danes to the Reign of George IV, with some account of the Ring Money, numerous illustrations, 4to, half bound. Cork, 1839

1018 Ruding. Rev. R.—Annals of the Coinage of Great Britain and its Dependencies from the Earliest Period of Authentic History to the Reign of Victoria, 3 vols. 4to, cloth. London, 1840

1019 Dickeson. M. W.—The American Numismatical Manual of the Currency or Money of the Aborigines and Colonial State and United States Coins, with Historical and Descriptive Notices of each Coin or Series, illustrated by 19 plates of fac-similes, 4to, cloth. Phila., 1859

1020 Crosby. S. S.—The Early Coins of America and the Laws Governing their Issue, comprising also descriptions of the Washington Pieces, the Anglo-American Tokens, many Pieces of Unknown Origin of the 17th and 18th Centuries, and the First Patterns of the United States Mint, profusely illustrated, in 12 numbers, complete, 4to. Boston, 1873

1021 Henfrey. H. M.—Numismata Cromwelliana, or the Medallic History of Oliver Cromwell, illustrated by his Coins, Medals and Seals, with numerous autotype illustrations, 4 numbers, complete, 4to. London, 1875

1022 De Strada. Octavii—De Vitis Imperatorom et Cæsarom Romanorom, Tam Accidentaliom qoam Orientaliom, Necnon vxorom et Liberorom Eorom, Item Tyrannorum Omnium, qui dincrsis Emporibus Romanum Imperium attentare and occupare conati sunt; Indeá C. Jolio Cæsare primo Monarcha, &c., numerous illustrations, folio, vellum. Francofurti, 1615

1023 American Journal of Numismatics and Bulletin of the American Numismatic and Archaeological Society, numerous illustrations, May, 1866, to October, 1877, inclusive, 78 numbers, consecutive. New York.

1024 Eckfeldt & Du Bois' Manual of Gold and Silver Coins of all Nations, struck within the Past Century, showing their History and Legal Basis, and their Actual Weight, Fineness and Value, chiefly from Original and Recent Essays by J. R. Eckfeldt & W. E. Du Bois, numerous illustrations, 4to, half mor. Phila., 1842

1025 The Sauri Britannic seu Museum Numarium Conplexum Numos Graecos, et Latinos Omnis Metalli et Formæ nesdum editos depictos et descriptos a Nicolas Francisco Haym, illustrated, 2 vols. 4to, paper and half calf. Vindobonæ.

1026 Snowden. Jas. Ross.—Description of the Medals of Washington, of National and Miscellaneous Medals, and of other Objects of Interest in the Museum of the Mint, illustrated by 79 fac-simile engravings, imperial 8vo, cloth. Phila., 1861

1027 Dubois. W. E.—Prevention of a Fraud upon our Gold Coins, 8vo, paper. Boston, 1874

1028 Description of Medals of Washington in the collection of W. S. Appleton, imperial, 8vo, paper. Boston, 1873

1029 Le Numismate Bulletin Periodique, accompagné d'un Catalogue de Médailles et Monnaies, Grecques Romaines du Moyen Age et des Temps Modernes, illustrated, 8vo, paper. Paris.

1030 Hickcox. Jno. H.—An Historical Account of American Coinage, illustrated, 8vo, large, paper, uncut. Albany, 1858

☞ 300 Copies printed : 5 copies only on large paper.

1031 Madden. F. W.—History of Jewish Coinage and of Money in the Old and New Testament, with 254 wood cuts and a plate of alphabets, by F. W. Fairholt, 8vo, half Roxburghe. London, 1864

1032 Snowden. J. R.—Description of Ancient and Modern Coins in the Cabinet Collection at the Mint of the United States, illustrated, 8vo, cloth. Phila., 1860

1033 Bushnell. Chas. I.—An Arrangement of Tradesmen's Cards, Political Tokens; also, Election Medals, Medalettes, &c, current in the United States of America, illustrated, 8vo, paper, uncut. New York, 1858

1034 Felt. Jno. B.—An Historical Account of Massachusetts Currency, illustrated, 8vo, cloth. Boston, 1839

1035 Akerman. Jno. Y.—Numismatic Illustrations of the Narrative Portions of the New Testament, illustrated, 8vo, cloth. London, 1846

1036 Burn. J. H.—Descriptive Catalogue of the London Traders' Tavern and Coffee-House, Tokens current in the Seventeenth Century presented to the Corporation Library, by H. B. H. Beaufoy, portrait of Beaufoy and Rich. Whitington, 8vo, cloth. London, 1855

1037 Akerman. Jno. Y.—A Numismatic Manual, illustrated, 8vo, cloth. London, 1840

1038 Akerman. Jno. Y.—Coins of the Romans relating to Britain described and illustrated, 8vo, cloth. London, 1844

1039 Akerman. J. Y.—Descriptive Catalogue of Rare and Unedited Roman Coins, from the Earliest Period of the Roman Coinage to the extinction of the Empire under Constantinus Paleologos, with numerous plates from the originals, 2 vols., 8vo, half bound. London, 1834

1040 Grasse. J. G. T.—Handbuck der Alten Numismatik von den Altesten Zeiten bis auf Constantin d. Gr., 1 vol., text; 1 vol., plates, (fac-simile,) printed in silver and gold, 2 vols., 8vo, half mor. Leipzig, 1854

1041 Hawkins. Edw'd—The Silver Coins of England, Arranged and Described, with Remarks on British Money Previous to the Saxon Dynasty, numerous illustrations, 8vo, half roan. London, 1841

1042 Eckfeldt and Du Bois—New Varieties of Gold and Silver Coins, Counterfeit Coins and Bullion, with Mint Values, by J. R. Eckfeldt and W. E. Du Bois, 8vo, cloth. New York, 1852

1043 The Institutes of the Numismatic Society of London, 1836–'39, illustrated, 8vo, half morocco, gilt, gilt top. London.

1044 The Numismatic Journal, edited by Jno. Y. Akerman, June 1836, to April, 1838, illustrated, 2 vols. 8vo, half morocco, gilt top. London.

1045 The Numismatic Chronicle, edited by Jno. Y. Akerman, June, 1838, to January, 1842, illustrated, 2 vols. 8vo, half morocco, gilt top. London.

1046 The Numismatic Chronicle and Journal of the Numismatic Society, edited by J. Y. Akerman and W. S. W. Vaux, April, 1842, to January, 1858, illustrated, 16 vols. 8vo, half morocco, gilt tops. London.

1046½ The Numismatic Chronicle and Journal of the Numismatic Society, edited by W. S. W. Vaux, J. Evans, and L. W. Madden, new series, 1860, to Part III, 1877, inclusive, 6 vols. 8vo, gilt tops, 10 vols. unbound and 3 numbers.

☞ The above five numbers should go together, as they form a complete set up to October, 1877.

1047 Bushnell. Charles I.—An Historical Account of the First Three Business Tokens issued in the City of New York, 8vo, paper. New York, 1859

☞ Privately printed—only 50 copies. Presentation copy.

1048 Satterlee. A. H.—An Arrangement of Medals and Tokens struck in Honor of the Presidents of the United States, &c., 8vo, paper. New York, 1862

1049 Mason's Quarterly Coin Collector's Magazine, April, 1867, to October, 1872, wanting May, June and August, 1872, 62 numbers.

1050 The Canadian Antiquarian and Numismatic Journal for July, 1872, January, April and October, 1873, 4 numbers.

1051 Levy. M. A.—Geschichte der Judischen Munzen, illustrated, 8vo, paper. Breslau, 1862

1052 Pinder. M.—Die Beckerschen Falschen Munzen, illustrated, 8vo, paper. Berlin, 1843

1053 Another copy, 8vo, paper. Berlin, 1843

1054 Another copy, 8vo, paper. Berlin, 1843

1055 Von Steinbuchel. A.—Die Beckerschen Falschen Munzstampfel in Ausfuhrlichen Verzeichnissen, 8vo, paper. Wien, 1836

1056 Another copy, 8vo, boards. Wien, 1836

1057 Weibezahn. H.—Deutschlands Munzenheit mit Goldwahrung, illustrated, 8vo, paper. Leipzig, 1871

1058 Another copy, 8vo, paper. Leipzig, 1871

1059 Appleton. W. S.—Description of a Selection of Coins and Medals relating to America, exhibited to the Massachusetts Historical Society, 8vo, paper. Cambridge, 1870

1060 Leake. S. M.—An Historical Account of English Money, from the Conquest to the Present Time, 8vo, calf. London, 1745

1061 Hayes. Rich.—The Negotiators' Magazine; or, the Most Authentic Account of Monies, Weights and Measures of the Principal Places of Trade in the known World, 8vo, calf. London, 1764

1062 Pinkerton. Jno.—An Essay on Meda's; or, an Introduction to the Knowledge of Coins and Medals, especially those of Greece, Rome and Britain, illustrated, 8vo, calf. London, 1789

1062½ Hawkins. Edw.—The Silver Coins of England arranged and described, with Remarks on British Money previous to the Saxon Dynasties, numerous engravings, 8vo, half morocco, gilt top. London, 1841

1063 Bowring. Sir Jno.—The Decimal System in Numbers, Coins and Accounts, portraits, 12mo, cloth. London, 1854

1064 Eckhel. J.—Kurzgesaszte Unsangsgrunde Zur Alten Numismatik, illustrated, 8vo, boards. Wien, 1807

1065 Pinkerton's Essay upon Money and Coins, part I, 8vo. London, 1757

1066 Humphreys. H. A.—The Coin Collector's Manual, or Guide to the Numismatic Student in the Formation of a Cabinet of Coins, over 150 engravings on wood and steel, 2 vols. 12mo, cloth. London, 1869

1067 Cinder. Jas.—An Arrangement of Provincial Coins, Tokens and Medalettes issued in Great Britain, Ireland and the Colonies, frontispiece, 12mo, half calf, gilt, marbled edges. Ipswich, 1776

1068 Lengnich. C. B.—Bentrage zur Kenntnisz Seltener und Merkwurdiger Bucher mit besondrer Kuchsieht aus die Numismatik, erster Theil, 8vo, paper. Danzig, 1776

1069 Till. W.—An Essay on the Roman Denarius and English Silver Penny, with a List of English and Scotch Pennies, illustrated, 12mo, cloth. London, 1838

1070 Till. W.—Descriptive Particulars of English Coronation Medals, illustrated, 12mo, cloth. London, 1838

1071 The Regulating Silver Coin made Practicable and Easy to the Government and Subject, 8vo, calf. London, 1696

1072 Birchall. Sam'l—Descriptive List of the Provincial Copper Coins or Tokens issued between the years 1786 and 1796, 12mo, paper. Leeds, 1796

1073 The Coin Act, by Way of Dialogue, by J. C., 16mo, paper. London, 1781

1074 Till. W.—The Farthings of Queen Anne, frontispiece, 16mo, paper. London, 1837

1075 Du Bois. W. E.—Brief Account of the Collection of Coins belonging to the Mint of the United States, frontispiece, 16mo, paper. Phila., 1846

1076 Bruckmann. F. E.—Bibliotheca Numismatica, 12mo, boards. Wolffenbuttel, 1729

1077 Akerman. J. Y.—An Introduction to the Study of Ancient and Modern Coins, illustrated, 16mo, cloth. London, 1848

1078 Bollstandige's Thaler-Labinet, 8vo. bds. Leipzig, 1735

1079 The Virtuoso's Companion and Coin Collector's Guide, numerous illustrations, 12vo, half morocco. London, 1797

1080 Addison. Jos.—Dialogues upon the Usefulness of Ancient Medals, illustrated, 16mo, calf. London, 1746

1081 Lincoln's Catalogues of Ancient and Modern Coins and Medals for 1858 and 1861, 16mo, cloth. London.

1082 Ditto, 1861, 16mo, half calf. London.

1083 Catalogue of the Collection of Greek and large Brass Coins of E. Harwood, &c., neatly priced, 8vo, half calf.

1084 Catalogue of the W. Benson Collection of Coins and Medals, 1815, and several others, all neatly priced, 8vo, half calf.

1085 Catalogue of the Baron Bolland Collection Coins and Medals, 1841, and several others, neatly priced, 8vo, boards.

1086 Catalogue of the John Knight Collection of Coins and Medals, 1842, and several others, 8vo, half calf.

1087 Catalague of the J D. Cuff Collection of Coins and Medals, 1854, neatly priced, 8vo, half roan.

1088 Catalogue of the Rich. Miles Collection of Coins, 1854, priced, 8vo, boards.

1089 Catalogue of the Rev. Jos. W. Martin Collection of Coins, 1859, priced, 8vo, half bound.

1090 Catalogue of the Marmaduke Trattle Collection of Coins and Medals, 1832, with portrait, priced, 8vo, half calf.

1091 Catalogue of the Mr. S. Higgs Collection of Coins and Choice Library, 1830, neatly priced, 8vo, half calf.

1092 2 Catalogues of Coins and Medals, 8vo, boards.

1093 Catalogue of the H. O. Cureton Collection of Coins and Medals, 1851, and Catalogue of the Rev. T. F. Dymock Collection of Coins, 1858, both neatly priced, large paper 8vo, half bound.

M. THOMAS & SONS, AUCTIONEERS,
139 and 141 South Fourth St.

www.ingramcontent.com/pod-product-compliance
Lightning Source LLC
Chambersburg PA
CBHW021541270326
41930CB00008B/1322

* 9 7 8 3 7 4 2 8 0 2 2 7 9 *